# 1 MONTH OF
# FREE
# READING

## at

## www.ForgottenBooks.com

By purchasing this book you are
eligible for one month membership to
ForgottenBooks.com, giving you
unlimited access to our entire
collection of over 1,000,000 titles via
our web site and mobile apps.

To claim your free month visit:
www.forgottenbooks.com/free576373

ISBN 978-0-656-71436-0
PIBN 10576373

Forgotten Books is a registered trademark of FB &c Ltd.
Copyright © 2018 FB &c Ltd.
FB &c Ltd, Dalton House, 60 Windsor Avenue, London, SW19 2RR.
Company number 08720141. Registered in England and Wales.

For support please visit www.forgottenbooks.com

S. Hrg. 104-123

# HEARING ON THE REAUTHORIZATION OF THE SPACE PROGRAMS OF THE NATIONAL AERONAUTICS AND SPACE ADMINISTRATION, THE DEPARTMENT OF TRANSPORTATION, AND THE U.S. DEPARTMENT OF COMMERCE

# HEARING

BEFORE THE

## SUBCOMMITTEE ON SCIENCE, TECHNOLOGY, AND SPACE

OF THE

# COMMITTEE ON COMMERCE, SCIENCE, AND TRANSPORTATION UNITED STATES SENATE

ONE HUNDRED FOURTH CONGRESS

FIRST SESSION

MARCH 1, 1995

Printed for the use of the Committee on Commerce, Science, and Transportation

U.S. GOVERNMENT PRINTING OFFICE

89-307 CC          WASHINGTON : 1995

For sale by the U.S. Government Printing Office
Superintendent of Documents, Congressional Sales Office, Washington, DC 20402

S. HRG. 104-123

# HEARING ON THE REAUTHORIZATION OF THE SPACE PROGRAMS OF THE NATIONAL AERONAUTICS AND SPACE ADMINISTRATION, THE DEPARTMENT OF TRANSPORTATION, AND THE U.S. DEPARTMENT OF COMMERCE

Y 4. C 73/7: S. HRG. 104-123

Hearing on the Reauthorization of t...

# HEARING

BEFORE THE

## SUBCOMMITTEE ON SCIENCE, TECHNOLOGY, AND SPACE

OF THE

## COMMITTEE ON COMMERCE, SCIENCE, AND TRANSPORTATION

## UNITED STATES SENATE

ONE HUNDRED FOURTH CONGRESS

FIRST SESSION

MARCH 1, 1995

Printed for the use of the Committee on Commerce, Science, and Transportation

U.S. GOVERNMENT PRINTING OFFICE

89–307 CC      WASHINGTON : 1995

For sale by the U.S. Government Printing Office
Superintendent of Documents, Congressional Sales Office, Washington, DC 20402

# CONTENTS

# HEARING ON THE REAUTHORIZATION OF THE SPACE PROGRAMS OF THE NATIONAL AERONAUTICS AND SPACE ADMINISTRATION, THE DEPARTMENT OF TRANSPORTATION, AND THE U.S. DEPARTMENT OF COMMERCE

## WEDNESDAY, MARCH 1, 1995

U.S. SENATE,
SUBCOMMITTEE ON SCIENCE, TECHNOLOGY, AND SPACE
COMMITTEE ON COMMERCE, SCIENCE, AND TRANSPORTATION,
*Washington, DC.*

The committee met, pursuant to notice, at 9:33 a.m., in room SR–253, Russell Senate Office Building, Hon. Conrad Burns, chairman of the subcommittee, presiding.

Staff members assigned to this hearing: Louis C. Whitsett, staff counsel, and Timothy B. Kyger, professional staff member; and Patrick H. Windham, minority senior professional staff.

### OPENING STATEMENT OF SENATOR BURNS

Senator BURNS. We will call this hearing to order.

Thank you for your patience this morning. I am sorry. I am just a little bit late. It seems as though we do not have enough to do up here right now. When you look at the calendar, it is mind boggling how we are going to get all the territory covered in this next 30 days.

First of all, I want to welcome Mr. Dan Goldin, who is the director of NASA, and Frank Weaver, from the Department of Transportation, and all you folks from the Department of Commerce, the witnesses who are here today, on this hearing on NASA's $14.3 billion budget request, and the commercial space activities at the Transportation and Commerce Departments.

With the increase in pressure of budgets—of course, these are not easy times for NASA. We have to make some hard choices.

But under the administrator, Mr. Goldin, under your bold leadership, NASA appears to be ready to make those choices.

For the second straight year, the NASA budget request asks for less money than previous year's funding level. Equally significant, this budget request calls for $5 billion in cuts over the next 5 years.

Now, here in Congress we're struggling to reduce the deficit so NASA's willingness to tighten its belt is really good news.

However, in cutting the costs, we do not want to jeopardize some very, very important parts of NASA, and one of those would be safety, or lose the significant content of the mission. NASA still has the responsibility to carry out its core missions in space exploration, in space science, aeronautics, and, of course, other areas.

To achieve $5 billion in budget reductions, NASA will truly need to reinvent itself. It will have to pare down its civil servant and contractor work force, close unnecessary facilities, eliminate redundant activities, and develop more efficient operations.

Just nibbling around the margins will not be enough. A radical restructuring of NASA will probably be required, and, in fact, I understand that an internal NASA study appears to be moving toward that conclusion.

We may have to face the harsh economic and political reality that the present structure of 12 NASA-supported field centers in their current configuration may be outmoded, and the need may be for change.

It may mean employing more efficient management systems. I do not have all the answers, but we must place all the reasonable options on the table to permit thoughtful consideration by not only NASA, but the policymakers here on the Hill.

I must emphasize, though, that this latest round of cuts takes NASA right down to the bone. To cut further without sacrificing safety would require canceling programs.

We cannot sacrifice safety, and I cannot emphasize that enough. I am hopeful that it will not be necessary, and that we could proceed with completing the programs in the current plan of operation.

In reviewing NASA's 1996 budget, it does appear that the agency has cut costs without sacrificing content, but there is still a $4 billion problem in the years of 1997 through the year 2000. That has not been resolved yet.

Hopefully, this problem can be resolved without cutting major programs or without having a delay in starting some very important programs that are on the drawing boards now, like the reusable launch vehicle effort, which is aimed to eventually build a replacement for the decades-old space shuttle.

Nevertheless, I am disappointed that NASA did not request the money for new wind tunnels. We understand what the problem is there. Because the wind tunnel money, I think, was not included, the $400 million already appropriated last year for that purpose cannot be released.

The U.S. commercial aircraft industry is one of the remaining industries in this country in which we have a very, very positive balance of trade.

If we are to maintain the preeminence of the United States in aerospace, we must build the research infrastructure to test the next-generation aircraft.

Without wind tunnels, U.S. aircraft manufacturers will have to go to Europe to do their testing, and I think we can agree that that just does not do a lot for our position of competition in the U.S. industrial world.

I also note that the space station receives full funding. For many people, NASA's success is measured by the progress of its $30 billion space station program. It is not surprising given that the space station is easily NASA's most expensive and highly publicized project.

I personally believe in the space station, because if past space missions are any indication, it will lead to greater understanding of the fundamental physics, chemistry, and biological processes, and generate new scientific and technological breakthroughs, things that we take for granted, like the new direct television satellite technology that we're enjoying now, even insulin pumps, microcomputers, are all direct results of the NASA space mission.

While I support the space station, its reliance on Russian participation obviously raises some very serious concerns.

I fully acknowledge Russia's skill and experience gained from many years of operating a series of space stations, including the current space station, Mir, but I am also concerned about the program's dependence on Russian launches, hardware, infrastructure, and personnel.

Congressional supporters of the space station would like some assurance that if the Russians are forced to pull out, for whatever reason, the space station program would still be able to remain on track.

With regard to the initiative aimed at replacing the shuttle, it is long overdue. NASA's shuttle orbiters use 1970's technology that is less advanced than that of your average commercial airplane. Moreover, it costs over $400 million per launch to fly.

NASA's reusable launch vehicle is a praiseworthy attempt to bring the shuttle program into the new high-tech age. Most significant, however, is the fact that NASA is stressing industry participation for the construction of any new test or operational vehicle.

This approach should both reduce the cost to the taxpayer and ensure the development of a vehicle relevant to the aerospace industry's needs.

We also need to consider the improvements in our present shuttle program. Aside from NASA's ongoing activities to improve the shuttle orbiters, I'm very interested in the idea of placing the shuttle program under one contractor, a move that could reduce the bureaucracy and trim the costs by ten to twenty percent, and the various privatization proposals that are now being debated.

One point that we need to stress is that NASA programs must be relevant to the needs of the taxpayers that fund them. NASA should touch the lives of all Americans, not just the ones living in those areas where NASA facilities are located.

For this reason, we must give proper attention to NASA's activities like the space grant programs and EPSCOR programs that help fund important research at many colleges in rural states, like my state of Montana.

Also, I'd like to stress the importance of NASA's education, outreach, and technology transfer programs for rural America.

Finally, I am also looking forward to the testimony of the Department of Transportation and the Department of Commerce witnesses about commercial space industry. The global markets for remote sensing satellites, communication satellites, and commercial launches have unlimited potential.

Rural states like Montana have a special interest in communication satellites dedicated to wireless communications. Wireless technology will give our rural states access to health care, education, and other applications, and, of course, it will play a huge role, I believe, in the information highway, without the need to spend billions on new wired infrastructure.

So let me again welcome our distinguished panel this morning. The subcommittee looks forward to taking their testimony.

[The prepared statement of Senator Burns follows:]

## PREPARED STATEMENT OF SENATOR BURNS

Let me welcome everyone to our hearing today on NASA's $14.3 billion budget request and the commercial space activities at the Transportation and Commerce Departments. With the increasing pressure to cut budgets, these are hard times for NASA and hard choices must be made. But under Administrator Dan Goldin's bold leadership, NASA appears ready to make those choices.

For the second straight year, the NASA budget request asks for less money than the previous year's funding level. Equally significant, this budget request calls for $5 billion in cuts over the next five years. Here in Congress, we are struggling to reduce the federal deficit, so NASA's willingness to tighten its belt is good news. However, in cutting costs, we do not want to jeopardize safety or lose significant content. NASA still has a responsibility to carry out its core missions in space exploration, space science, aeronautics, and other areas.

To achieve $5 billion in budget reductions, NASA will truly need to "reinvent itself." It will have to pare down its civil servant and contractor work force, close unnecessary or consolidation facilities, eliminate redundant activities, and develop more efficient operations. Just nibbling at the margins will not be enough. A radical restructuring of NASA is probably required and, in fact, I understand that an internal NASA study appears to be moving towards that conclusion.

We may have to face the harsh economic and political reality that the present structure of 12 NASA supported field centers in their current configuration may be outmoded and need to change. It may mean employing more efficient management systems. I do not have all the answers, but we must place all reasonable options on the table for thoughtful consideration by policy makers.

I must emphasize, though, that this latest round of cuts takes NASA "down to the bone." To cut further, without sacrificing safety, would require canceling programs. We cannot sacrifice safety! I am hopeful that will not be necessary, and that we can proceed with completing the programs in the current operating plan.

In reviewing NASA's FY96 budget, it does appear that the agency has cut costs without sacrificing content, but there is still a $4 billion problem in the years 1997-2000 unresolved. Hopefully, this problem can be resolved without cutting major programs or without having to delay starting some very important new programs like the Reusable Launch Vehicle effort, which is aimed at eventually building a replacement for the decades-old Space Shuttle.

Nevertheless, I am disappointed that NASA did not request money for new wind tunnels. Because the wind tunnel money was not included, the $400 million already appropriated last year for that purpose cannot be released. The U.S. commercial aircraft industry is one of the only remaining industries with a positive balance of trade. If we are to maintain U.S. preeminence in aerospace, we must build the research infrastructure to test our next-generation aircraft. Without the wind tunnels, U.S. aircraft manufacturers will have to go to Europe to do their testing. We can all agree that this situation does not bode well for U.S. industrial competitiveness.

I also note that Space Station receives full funding. For many people, NASA's success is measured by the progress of the $30 billion Space Station program. This is not surprising given that Space Station is easily NASA's most expensive and highly publicized project. I personally believe in Space Station because, if past space missions are any indication, it will lead to a greater understanding of fundamental physics, chemistry, and biological processes and generate new scientific and technological breakthroughs. Things we take for granted like the new "Direct TV" satellite technology, insulin pumps, and microcomputers are all the direct result of NASA's space missions.

While I support Space Station, its reliance on Russian participation obviously raises some serious concerns. I fully acknowledge Russia's skill and experience gained from many years of operating a series of space stations, including its current spacecraft, "Mir." But I am also concerned about the program's dependence on Russian launches, hardware, infrastructure, and personnel. Congressional supporters of Space Station would like some assurance that, if the Russians are forced to pull out—for whatever reason—the Space Station program would still be able to remain on track.

With regard to the initiative aimed at replacing the Shuttle, it is long overdue. NASA's Shuttle orbiters use 1970s technology that is less advanced than that of your average commercial airplane. Moreover, it costs over $400 million per launch to fly. NASA's Reusable Launch Vehicle is a praiseworthy attempt to bring the Shuttle program into our new high-tech age. Most significant, however, is the fact that NASA is stressing industry participation in the construction of any new test or operational vehicle. This approach should both reduce the cost to the taxpayer and insure the development of a vehicle relevant to the aerospace industry's needs.

We also need to consider improvements in our present Shuttle program. Aside from NASA's ongoing activities to improve the Shuttle orbiters, I am very interested in the idea of placing the Shuttle program under one contractor—a move that could reduce the bureaucracy and trim costs by 10 to 20 percent—and the various privatization proposals that are being debated.

One point that we need to stress is that NASA programs must be relevant to the needs of the taxpayers that fund them. NASA should touch the lives of all Americans not just those living in areas with NASA facilities. For this reason, we must give proper attention to NASA activities like the Space Grant program and "EPSCOR"—programs that help fund important research at many colleges in rural states like Montana. Also, I would like to stress the importance of NASA's education, outreach, and technology transfer programs for rural states.

Finally, I am also looking forward to the testimony from our DoT and DoC witnesses about the commercial space industry. The global markets for remote sensing satellites, communications satellites, and commercial launches have unlimited potential. Rural states like Montana have a special interest in the communications satellites dedicated to "wireless" communications. Wireless technology will give our rural states access to the health care, educational, and other applications of the "information superhighway" without the need to spend billions on brand-new "wired" infrastructure.

Let me again welcome our distinguished panel of witnesses to the Subcommittee and I look forward to hearing their testimony.

I will say that when we go through the reauthorization process, that any testimony that you would like to be made part of the record, we will hold that record open until all your information is complete.

So I thank you for coming this morning. I recognize Senator Hutchison. She has a statement at this time.

## STATEMENT OF SENATOR HUTCHISON

Senator HUTCHISON. Thank you, Mr. Chairman.

Let me just say that I had the privilege last week to go to NASA with Mr. Goldin and look at some of the new programs and see what is being done, and really put in perspective the importance of these science projects for future technology, future industries, future jobs in this country.

There is no doubt that Mr. Goldin is doing everything possible to keep the programs and run the operation in a lean and mean way, or kinder or gentler, I don't know, but it seems like it's getting leaner by the day.

I think we have to continue to put the long-term vision in our equation. Sometimes I think in our efforts to cut the budget, we look at the size of a project rather than the importance of a project.

Our big science research budget used to be over 5 percent of the Federal budget. Today it's less than 2 percent. That is going to take a toll on the long term in this country.

So I hope that today in your testimony that you will talk about what you are doing, but also how you are working within the constraints of lower budgets, and how you are trying to handle the programs without cutting out any specific program that has merit.

So I know it is a challenge. I appreciate the visit last week. Mr. Chairman, we are looking forward to your coming NASA as well, because I think you will also really see firsthand what we are doing to stay in the forefront of technology and science in this country, if you could come and visit us.

Senator BURNS. Well, we hope to make the trip pretty quick, that is, when the load lightens up here. I do not know when that is going to be.

Senator HUTCHISON. Tell me, when do we start having fun, Mr. Chairman.

Senator BURNS. Yes. That is right.

Director Goldin, good morning to you. Thank you for coming this morning.

Welcome, Dr. Cordova and Mr. Peterson. We look forward to your testimony, and we will turn the microphone over to you. Thank you for coming.

PREPARED STATEMENT OF SENATOR HOLLINGS

This morning's hearing comes at a critical point in the history of the U.S. space program. NASA has great ambitions but less and less funding. It is not clear that it can accomplish all that it wishes.

Moreover, all Federal programs deserve scrutiny in this new era of constrained Federal budgets, intense global economic competition, and no Cold War. We must focus limited resources on top priorities. And as in all other areas of government, we must ask whether our aeronautics and space activities truly meet today's national needs. Are NASA program's focused enough on long-term support for the economically vital aircraft industry? What is the best way for the Federal Government to work with American companies to lower costs in commercial space activities? What is the appropriate role of human space flight in the post-Code War world? These are questions Congress now faces.

I am pleased that the Science Subcommittee is holding today's hearing. I look forward to reviewing the testimony, and look forward to continuing to discuss these issues with my colleagues.

## STATEMENT OF DANIEL S. GOLDIN, ADMINISTRATOR, NATIONAL AERONAUTICS AND SPACE ADMINISTRATION; ACCOMPANIED BY DR. FRANCE CORDOVA, CHIEF SCIENTIST; MALCOLM PETERSON, DEPUTY COMPTROLLER; AND CHARLES KENNEL, ASSOCIATE ADMINISTRATOR FOR MISSION TO PLANET EARTH

Mr. GOLDIN. Thank you, Mr. Chairman. I would like to submit my formal testimony for the record, and just give a few brief statements to summarize what is in that testimony.

Senator BURNS. Without objection. We will make your full statement a part of the record.

Mr. GOLDIN. I would just like to indicate that if you did not know, Dr. France Cordova is the chief scientist of NASA, and Mal Peterson is the NASA Comptroller, and they will support me in my testimony here.

I would like to start off by saying how proud I am of the NASA team. This is a team of explorers, pioneers, and inventors, people who are not afraid to go to the frontier, people who are not afraid to take risks, because they are concerned about future generations of America. They are concerned about the vision.

They will take bold risks on noble tasks and do things that stir the mind and lift the spirits for all Americans, and God only knows, we need a little bit of that in these times. They are going to blaze the trail for future Americans, the children.

As I travel around the country and I ask people what is important to you, the No. 1 response is "I want my children to have a better life than I had."

And this is what we are all about at NASA. This last year at NASA has been just stunning in terms of accomplishments. Let me just name a few. We had a rendezvous with the Russian Mir space station and the U.S. shuttle.

To give you a sense about the ability of our people when questioned by the press, Commander Jim Weatherby was asked, "Are you concerned? You know, the Russians are concerned about the U.S. shuttle rendezvousing with the Mir space station." Do you know what he said? "They haven't seen me fly. I am really good." This is the spirit of NASA. This is what we are all about. No one is afraid of taking risks. We do things sensibly, but we go to the limits.

The space station, we debated it for 10 years, and last year we built hardware, 26,500 pounds of hardware, and we held the launch date. One year expenditure, 1 year progress, the launch date holds.

This is a team that is on fire. We did it with a management team of 300 people, not 2,000 people, because we turned responsibility over to a prime contractor. In fact, the space station downsized 5,000 jobs, and we made more progress las year than we made in the past.

The Hubble rescue mission was unbelievable. It built confidence that we know how to do EVAs. It built confidence that we could do bold science. And the results have been stunning, in terms of discoveries on black holes and new galaxies.

We updated the U.S. weather spacecraft. The GOES spacecraft is now on station, and NASA handed it over to NOAA. Americans can now get a much better understanding of the weather and storm warnings.

And not only do we have technical achievements, but management achievements. We signed up to a 30 percent budget cut over the last 2 years, and we have proved the concept that less is more.

We did not cut the heart and soul out of NASA, we cut unnecessary tasks and bureaucracy, and we are blazing a path to do new things.

I might also say but a few years ago, overruns were a problem at NASA. Of the 16 major science and development programs, the average reduction in the cost of those programs was–5.3 percent, and there was only one program that had a significant growth, and that was the GGS program at 13 percent.

But people understand that when you hit the 15 percent barrier at NASA, you must defend why you should not be canceled. So we are on track management-wise.

We announced a near asteroid rendezvous. Four missions to Mars for the price of one, with two landers and robots, and orbiters.

Yesterday, we announced the bold chemical prospector of the moon, to search for chemical resources on the moon, and perhaps to see if there is water at the poles of the moon, so future explorers could have it. It is $59 million for the total price of that mission.

Two spacecraft universities, non-conventional, $24 million and two complete spacecraft programs. So we are changing the way we are doing business.

The fiscal 1996 budget is robust. We are starting the New Millennium spacecraft, which will allow us to have dozens of launches a year instead of two launches a year. Instead of spacecraft at $600 million average price, NASA is going to have spacecraft under $100 million average price.

We took up your challenge, Mr. Chairman, and we are going to give America a new series of launch vehicles that will be leap frog, not me too technologies, not technologies that protect industry by protecting jobs of today, but jobs for tomorrow.

We applaud the leadership of President Clinton in his bold move to ask us to reduce another $5 billion. We view this not as a problem, but as an opportunity to set the next stage for exploration in the twenty-first century.

We are going to have a revolutionary overhaul of NASA. The American people spoke in the 1994 election, and they said they want less government, but they want the government that remains to be more effective.

They want to measure us on output. No longer will we measure the vitality of the NASA program by how many dollars we get. We want America to judge us by what we do for the American public. We have two choices. We could protect infrastructure and cut programs, or we can cut infrastructure, and expand programs. We chose the second path.

This second path is very, very painful, because it will involve the displacement of jobs of people who have done a wonderful task, but it is the right thing. American industry downsized, and they are more flexible, and NASA can do the same thing.

But we need one level of support from this committee. We need stability in the 1995 and the 1996 budgets to allow us to maintain the safety, to allow us to treat the employees with dignity, and not just push employees out and not treat them with the dignity they have deserved. We need time to make adjustments and make up front investments so we can get the costs out later. So we are committed to cutting $5 billion, but we need stability in the next 2 years to make that happen.

It is a very difficult task, but it is the right thing to do. I feel pain and anguish for the employees who are going to be involved, but we must make NASA more agile, more mobile.

We have to get out of the operations business. We have to get out of the business of telling industry how to do things, and be less directive and enabling, to open the space frontier.

This is exciting. We are making the way for the new future, and I want to applaud the leadership and vision of President Clinton in allowing us to move forward to the space frontier.

Thank you very much.

[The prepared statement of Mr. Goldin follows:]

National Aeronautics and
Space Administration

Hold for Release Until
Presented by Witness

March 1, 1995

# Subcommittee on Science, Technology, and Space

# Committee on Commerce, Science, and Transportation

# United States Senate

Statement by:
**Daniel S. Goldin**
Administrator

104th Congress

**Statement of**
**Daniel S. Goldin**
**Administrator**
**National Aeronautics and Space Administration**

**before the**

**Subcommittee on Science, Technology and Space**
**Committee on Commerce, Science and Transportation**
**United States Senate**

**March 1, 1995**

NASA is an investment in America's future.

We do what no other part of government can do. We boldly expand frontiers in air and space to benefit the quality of life on Earth. We seek to unravel the mysteries of the universe and, in the process, we make the country stronger and more competitive.

The FY 1996 budget request of $14.26 billion will allow us to continue to fulfill that promise (Figure 1). We will deliver a strong aeronautics and space program that's relevant to America.

That's the good news.

The tough news is that we will make **fundamental changes** at NASA to absorb future cuts.

We've already cut our five-year budget plan by 30% since 1993. We've already reduced our support contracts and downsized our workforce. We've already eliminated low-priority programs. Given all that, the need to find an additional $5 billion calls for sweeping changes at NASA. We must rethink the entire Agency (Figure 2 & 3).

**Make no mistake. When this is over, NASA will be profoundly different. We're going to restructure the Agency. But the NASA that emerges will be better than ever.**

We have a vision for NASA, and a road map for change.

11

First and foremost, we're going to revolutionize the structure of NASA. Our workforce. Our relationship with our contractors. Our facilities. In a word, everything.

In the past, one of the ways we've dealt with cuts is to trim NASA's structure. Trimming won't do it anymore. The Agency must be completely restructured. The new NASA will be fundamentally different from the old.

We're going to use seven basic principles to restructure:

o    One, we'll cut out duplication and overlaps and consolidate.

o    Two, if we don't have to do it ourselves, we won't. Maybe a university or the private sector should be doing a function NASA's doing now. We'll turn it over to them.

o    Three, we'll change the way we work with prime contractors. We'll do less. They'll do more.

o    Four, we'll privatize and commercialize wherever appropriate. We'll work with industry on the front end and then get out of the way. That's exactly what we're going to do with the Reusable Launch Vehicle Technology Program.

o    Five, we'll work to get regulations changed so we can do business differently and empower the Agency to work more efficiently and effectively with contractors.

o    Six, we'll cut way back on NASA's ever growing operations budget by turning these activities over to the private sector, and return NASA to the cutting edge of research and development.

o    Seven, we will emphasize objective contracting. This is a critical procurement reform. Contractors will be given a statement of work that calls for a specific product that's deliverable to NASA by a firm deadline. We want NASA to enable the aerospace business, not to direct it. Objective contracting enables companies to align their commercial aerospace business with their NASA-related work. This may require policy and regulatory changes discussed above.

Using these principles, we want to make the full $5 billion reduction through restructuring. Cutting our workforce, cutting on-site contractors, cutting facilities. This will be painful. It means NASA employees will lose their jobs. Contractors working at NASA, and at their own offices, will lose their jobs (Figure 4).

I wish we could reinvent NASA without any disruption to any employee. I wish it were easy. But it isn't. We are offering a second buyout, which should help move us toward our targets. We hope to make all of the cuts through restructuring. If our analysis shows we can't, then and only then will we cancel programs.

But I do want to emphasize an important change that affects our programs. The way we're evaluating them now is profoundly different from how we've done it in the past. We used to measure the Agency's vitality by the level of its budget. Not any more. We're going to measure our success by output, not input. We'll judge our success by the science, the R&D, the **results** of what we do, not by the dollars going in.

The kind of sweeping changes this budget calls for are new. But doing things more efficiently and effectively with less money is not at all new at NASA. We already have begun a revolution. We have been in the vanguard of the President's and Vice President's reinvention challenge.

The White House recently announced a second phase of the National Performance Review to examine the basic missions of government. We're already doing that. We're in the middle of a top-to-bottom review of the Agency to determine where to cut. We're looking at everything we do. Everything is on the table.

o     In October, we began a zero base review of our civil servants and contractors.

o     Two teams are reviewing Shuttle operations. One began last September and the other last month. They're looking for ways to significantly cut costs while achieving safety equal to or better than today's level. Safety governs everything we do. It's our top priority.

o     We're involved in the Federal Lab Review, to see how our R&D labs can be more efficient and effective. This review began in September.

13

We'll also make NASA less of an operations Agency and more of an R&D Agency. This process begins in FY 1996. Let me turn now to some of the specifics of the FY 1996 budget:

o   We intend to maintain our critical major activities.

o   We're continuing the "better, faster cheaper" revolution (Figure 5). We're replacing large, complex spacecraft with smaller, less expensive missions with shorter development times:

   o   Mars/Pathfinder,
   o   Near Earth Asteroid Rendezvous,
   o   Mars Surveyor,
   o   Explorer missions, and
   o   Smallsat program (Lewis and Clark  missions).

o   Our Mission to Planet Earth program has made progress in understanding the global environment. We have found a way to measure sea level change from space. We have an objective way of measuring global temperature change from space. Our airplanes are studying the last unpolluted air mass on Earth. This air mass, which is over the central Pacific Ocean, is relatively untouched by human activity. This information will give us a yardstick by which to measure the effects of an industrial world on the atmosphere. And there's much more to come. The Earth Observing System (EOS) will make the first integrated observations of the climate beginning in 1998. EOS results will help scientists create advanced computer models of the interactions between air, land, water and life. These results will also be made available to farmers, foresters, fishermen, resource planners, educators, and the public. Furthermore, we hope these efforts will spur the growth of a whole new remote sensing industry and give U.S. businesses a competitive edge in the expanding world-wide remote sensing market.

o   We're continuing to work to improve Shuttle safety. Safety is our highest priority. With the goal of enhancing overall safety, this budget includes funds for modifications to the Main Engine, Orbiter and Redesigned Solid Rocket Booster. The Shuttle continues to perform brilliantly. The rendezvous with the Mir earlier this month was a dazzling feat. The docking mission planned for May will be a technological miracle and a powerful symbol of the new cooperation between the U.S. and Russia.

o  We'll continue to move ahead with vital aeronautics programs, like the High Speed Research Program. This is cutting-edge technology. It has the potential to create 150,000 jobs and $250 billion in revenue.

o  We're also moving full speed ahead with the Advanced Subsonic Transport program. We'll be working with industry to develop high-payoff technologies that support a safe, environmentally friendly, highly productive global air transportation system. In FY 1996, we've redirected some resources to emphasize two areas our customers say are critical — air traffic management technologies and affordable design and manufacturing.

   o  We're continuing our exciting work in the High Performance Computing and Communications Program. Today's supercomputers can do between 10 and 100 billion calculations a second. Our goal is one trillion in the next few years, and a quadrillion in the next 15 years. Industry will take this technology and run with it.

   o  Just as we promised last year, we're increasing space science funding (Figure 6). We'll be starting some exciting new science programs:

      o  We're staging a revolution with the New Millennium spacecraft. There's no other word for it. This is a brand new era in spacecraft design. These small, agile spacecraft will be built on a bench, not in a high bay area. They'll be about a tenth of the cost and about a tenth of the weight of today's spacecraft but with the same high quality science. They're like nothing that's ever been done before.

      o  We're starting a new era in infrared astronomy with The Stratospheric Observatory for Infrared Astronomy (SOFIA), and The Space Infrared Telescope Facility (SIRTF). We hope to reveal the answers to outstanding questions about planetary disks, brown dwarfs, and the most luminous galaxies.

      o  More Discovery missions -- we'll do one a year, insuring that university scientists *and their students* are on a fast-track to knowledge about our Solar System.

      o  And we'll do the Rosetta mission. This is an example of how we're doing business differently at NASA. Through international cooperation, we'll do this mission for much less than the original comet rendezvous we'd planned. ESA

is taking the lead. We'll rendezvous with a comet and
deliver landers to the surface. One lander will be American,
developed with French participation. And one will be
German.

o   This budget request also lays the groundwork for the next 20
years in space exploration. We'll be developing the tools of the
future.

o   I've already mentioned the New Millennium spacecraft. It's
one of the most exciting ways we're preparing for the future.

o   The Reusable Launch Vehicle Technology Program is
another ground breaker. The Shuttle is a magnificent and
versatile spacecraft. But it's time to look to the next era in
space. Reusable Launch Vehicles should make access to
space affordable and open up the space frontier to industry
and entrepreneurs.

And the way we're working with industry is the wave of the future.
We're going to work with industry to resolve high-risk development issues and
then get out of the way. Industry will build and operate the launch vehicles. In
the future, I expect that NASA will be just another customer for commercial
launch services.

These are some of the highlights of our FY 1996 budget. We have a strong
program that builds on the spectacular successes of this past year.

We had a record year in FY 1994, with tremendous successes in three areas:
we continued to transform the way NASA operates; we performed stellar
missions; and we responded to Congressional direction to increase funding for
space science.

Let me start with the first area. We continued to revolutionize NASA:

oWe responded to specific recommendations to the Agency from the National
Performance Review. These recommendations varied from improving
our technology transfer to making program management more
effective.

o   We implemented an award fee initiative that builds in cost controls
and holds contractors accountable for performance.

oWe dramatically simplified our process for selecting and awarding contracts
of under half a million dollars a year.

o      In partnership with contractors, we started an initiative to improve cost control. We set up another process to simplify and enhance major procurement selection.

o      We completely changed the structure of the international Space Station program and streamlined its management. This is a model for our new way of doing business. We overhauled the Station from top to bottom. We selected a single prime contractor, Boeing, and we now have a signed contract. We established a single program office at the NASA Johnson Space Center. We built in real incentives for cost and technical performance and real penalties for delays.

Now let me turn to the second area -- our outstanding program accomplishments in 1994.

o      I mentioned the Station management. We also built 26,500 pounds of hardware. Thanks to stable funding, we are building the Station. We're not debating it anymore. We're doing it. Further, we solidified Russian participation and signed a $400 million contract for Russian space hardware, services and data. The Station is right on track.

o      The Shuttle program also was another incredible success. It accomplished seven highly productive science and technology missions in 1994. The first Russian cosmonaut flew aboard a U.S. spacecraft as we continued to prepare for visits to the Mir. All together, the Shuttle carried 42 astronauts to space, including crew members from Russia, Japan and the European Space Agency. They spent over 81 days in orbit.

o We did absolutely outstanding science last year:

o      For the first time ever, scientists now have decisive evidence of the existence of black holes, courtesy of the Hubble Space Telescope. Shortly after being repaired last December, Hubble was trained on the giant elliptical galaxy M87, located 50 million light years away in the constellation Virgo. Hubble's observation confirms more than two centuries of theory and conjecture about the reality of black holes.

o   Hubble data confirmed the existence of protoplanetary disks
    around newborn stars. This is the strongest evidence yet that
    the same process that formed the planets in our Solar System
    is common throughout the galaxy and, presumably, the
    universe.

o   After peering deep into space and far back in time, Hubble
    detected primordial helium in the early universe. This is
    important because it confirms one of the critical tenets of the
    Big Bang theory. It is one more important confirmation of our
    best guess as to how space and time formed.

o   This year, a strange new phenomenon known as upper
    atmospheric flashes was recorded for the first time. The
    Compton Gamma Ray Observatory contributed to this
    discovery. These flashes last only a few hundredths or
    thousandths of a second, and extend upward as high as 60
    miles. Some reach through the ozone layer to the ionosphere.
    It is thought that these flashes provide a link between Earth's
    lower atmosphere to events in the upper layers of our
    atmosphere.

o   The impact of Comet P/Shoemaker-Levy 9 with Jupiter in July
    was a seminal event for astronomers. Not only was the Near
    Earth Object Program able to detect the comet in 1993 and
    predict its eventual impact -- to the day -- but it also afforded
    an unprecedented campaign to observe this event from ground-
    based and space-based observatories. The observations
    acquired revealing data about the composition of comets and
    the composition of the Jovian atmosphere. The event itself was
    the subject of worldwide interest from the scientific community
    and the public.

o   The Galileo probe, enroute to Jupiter, confirmed that a tiny
    moonlet orbits the asteroid Ida. That moonlet was recently
    named Dactyl. The size of the asteroid Ida suggests that such
    moons may be more widespread than previously thought.

o   In April, NASA successfully launched the next-generation
    Geostationary Operational Environmental Satellite, GOES-8.
    The new weather satellite will enable forecasters to more
    accurately track and predict storms, including hurricanes. As
    the capabilities of the new satellite become operational,
    television viewers around the  country will notice sharper and
    more detailed images on their local weather forecasts.

o    Last year, NASA demonstrated two new techniques for
     observing the Earth from space. In April, and again in
     October, NASA flew a multi-frequency, multi-polarization
     radar, the most complex ever flown in space, to study ecology,
     water cycles, vegetation cover, oceanography, geology and
     volcanology. This was the first remote sensing observation of
     the Central African habitat of mountain gorillas, in an area
     now threatened by civil unrest in Rwanda. The second
     technique was demonstrated last week aboard the Space
     Shuttle. Known as lidar, for light detection and ranging,
     scientists used a laser beam to bounce off objects and used the
     reflected energy to make environmental observations of the
     planet.

o    Mission To Planet Earth is delivering more science every year.
     Results from our upper atmospheric research satellite indicate
     that ozone depletion is stabilizing -- the first sign the treaties
     are working. Topex/Poseidon made the first global
     measurements of sea level rise in 1994, and saw El Nino
     weather events in the making. Soon, we'll be able to predict
     rainy winters like the one California is having.

o    We also delivered on our commitment to Congress to increase
     funding for NASA's Space Science program by reallocating
     funds (Figure 7).

We clearly had some stunning successes last year. And we will in the future.
A new, restructured NASA will continue to strengthen the country and inspire
America's children.

We're an investment in the future.

Twenty years from now, America will have recaptured a portion of the 25%
market share in aviation the nation has lost over the last 25 years. We'll have
a domestic aviation industry second to none. It will produce a wide range of
highly competitive products that are quiet, environmentally compatible and
sustain hundreds of thousands of high-quality manufacturing jobs.

We will have mapped the entire Solar System. We will have gone past Pluto
and out to the Oort cloud, where the building blocks of creation are hidden.

We will have sent an armada of small spacecraft out into the Solar System.
And the information they send back will belong to everyone. Students, workers,
older Americans -- everyone -- will take part in these discoveries.

We'll take high-resolution pictures of planets — if they exist — within 30 to 50 light years of Earth. Wouldn't it be exciting if we found a blue planet with clouds, with carbon dioxide and oxygen out of equilibrium.

Children in science classes will operate robots on the Moon. High school students will analyze samples and put their results on the Internet.

We will restore people's link to nature through Earth observations and communications. We will understand much more about our own planet and global environment through Mission to Planet Earth.

While we learn how people can live and work in space, we will contribute to improving the quality of health care for old and young alike. Doctors will have enhanced data and new techniques. The combination of the unique research we do in space and the medical research done on the ground by NIH and others will be a powerful force for unlocking the mysteries of disease.

The possibilities for what we will have learned from the Station are incredible. We may have learned how people can live and work in space for long periods of time. We may have learned what we need to know to send humans to another planet. We will be planning the world's next destination in space.

All of these things are possible if we continue to revolutionize NASA. A strong, dynamic space and aeronautics program is an investment in America's children and the nation's future.

I want to close by thanking the President for his leadership. He's given us clear, forceful direction. He's asking us to do what's most important to Americans and do it for less money. In fact, he's asking us to change NASA as we know it.

I know there are many members of Congress who support that. They've told us much the same thing. To deliver a relevant program for less. And to overhaul the Agency to make that happen. And with your help, that's exactly what we're going to do.

And we do need your help to accomplish all this. The massive restructuring I have described will not be quick or easy. This is an undertaking that goes to the basics of the Agency's structure, and what we do will forever change NASA. The roles and missions of our Centers and Headquarters will change. Our workforce, our contractors, our facilities will change. It will take time, careful study and constant vigilance to maintain safety of flight and deliver on our program commitments while we do this.

NASA is a very special Agency. We must fly the Shuttle and do all of our missions safely. We need a controlled process for change that enables us to retain a critical balance of skills at NASA. Without that balance, we will not be able to make safety equal to or better than today's level. We also need a controlled, deliberate process in order to protect the human dignity of our employees. They need time to transition to new jobs. These are brilliant people — many of whom have left their mark not just on NASA but on the country. Further, as we phase out some of our activities, we will be exploring the possibility of turning them over to local communities. That could be good news for these areas because it may mean new jobs and industries, but this, too, will take careful planning if the process is to work smoothly.

We will need time to do all this right. We will also need the strong support of Congress and an appropriation at the level of the President's FY 1996 budget request -- $14.26 billion. The President's FY 1996 budget request enables us to deliver on our promise to you and to the Nation to deliver a vital program that helps position America for a successful, competitive 21st Century.

**The stability of this funding level -- both our current FY 1995 level and the President's FY 1996 budget request -- is essential. In addition to enabling us to preserve or enhance safety and protect the dignity of our employees, we'll need this funding to make the dramatic changes I've described. Moving employees, achieving new automation and many other aspects of restructuring cost money. These are one-time investments that will yield savings in the long run, but they do require upfront expenditures. While we will achieve some savings from our second buyout, this money will be needed for the cost of achieving the new, transformed NASA.**

We plan to work very closely with the distinguished Members of this Subcommittee and others in Congress. We intend to be a "user-friendly" Agency for Congress. I'm confident that, working together for the good of the Agency and the good of the country, we will continue the revolution that's already begun at NASA.

Thank you.

## NATIONAL AERONAUTICS & SPACE ADMINISTRATION

### FY 1996 BUDGET SUMMARY
### (MILLIONS OF DOLLARS)

| | 1994 | BUDGET PLAN 1995 | 1996 |
|---|---|---|---|
| **HUMAN SPACE FLIGHT** | **6,074.3** | **5,514.9** | **5,509.6** |
| SPACE STATION | 1,939.2 | 1,889.6 | 1,833.6 |
| US/RUSSIAN COOPERATIVE PROGRAM | 170.8 | 150.1 | 129.2 |
| SPACE SHUTTLE | 3,558.7 | 3,155.1 | 3,231.8 |
| PAYLOAD AND UTILIZATION OPERATIONS | 405.6 | 320.1 | 315.0 |
| **SCIENCE, AERONAUTICS AND TECHNOLOGY** | **5,792.5** | **5,943.6** | **6,006.9** |
| SPACE SCIENCE | 1,920.9 | 2,012.6 | 1,958.9 |
| LIFE AND MICROGRAVITY SCIENCES AND APPLICATIONS | 507.5 | 483.1 | 504.0 |
| MISSION TO PLANET EARTH | 1,068.0 | 1,340.1 | 1,341.1 |
| AERONAUTICAL RESEARCH AND TECHNOLOGY | 1,067.2 | 882.0 | 917.3 |
| SPACE ACCESS AND TECHNOLOGY | 562.4 | 642.4 | 705.6 |
| MISSION COMMUNICATION SERVICES | 581.0 | 481.2 | 461.3 |
| ACADEMIC PROGRAMS | 85.5 | 102.2 | 118.7 |
| **MISSION SUPPORT** | **2,667.4** | **2,589.2** | **2,726.2** |
| SAFETY, RELIABILITY AND QUALITY ASSURANCE | 34.3 | 38.7 | 37.6 |
| SPACE COMMUNICATION SERVICES | 248.2 | 226.5 | 319.4 |
| RESEARCH AND PROGRAM MANAGEMENT | 2,175.6 | 2,189.0 | 2,202.8 |
| CONSTRUCTION OF FACILITIES | 209.3 | 135.0 | 166.4 |
| **INSPECTOR GENERAL** | **14.7** | **16.0** | **17.3** |
| **NATIONAL AERONAUTICAL FACILITIES** | | **400.0** | |
| **TOTAL BUDGET AUTHORITY** | **14,548.9** | **14,463.7** | **14,260.0** |
| **TOTAL OUTLAYS** | **13,693.3** | **14,239.4** | **14,125.3** |

(FIGURE 1)

# FY 1996 PRESIDENT'S BUDGET

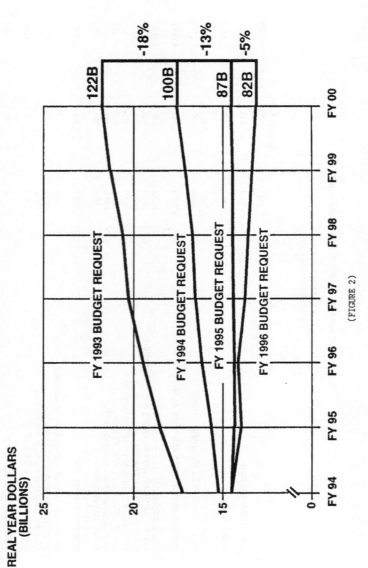

(FIGURE 2)

## FY 1996 PRESIDENT'S BUDGET
### MILLIONS OF DOLLARS

### HUMAN SPACE FLIGHT, SCIENCE, AERONAUTICS AND TECHNOLOGY, MISSION SUPPORT, AND INSPECTOR GENERAL APPROPRIATIONS

|  | FY 1994 | FY 1995 | FY 1996 | FY 1997 | FY 1998 | FY 1999 | FY 2000 |
|---|---|---|---|---|---|---|---|
| FY 1995 BUDGET REQUEST | 14,551 | 14,300 | 14,400 | 14,500 | 14,600 | 14,600 | 14,700 |
| CHANGE | -3 | -236 | -140 | -604 | -947 | -1,189 | -1,532 |
| FY 1996 BUDGET REQUEST | 14,549 | 14,064 | 14,260 | 13,896 | 13,653 | 13,411 | 13,168 |

### NATIONAL AERONAUTICAL FACILITIES APPROPRIATION

|  | FY 1995 |
|---|---|
| FY 1995 BUDGET REQUEST | --- |
| CHANGE | 400 |
| FY 1996 BUDGET REQUEST | 400 * |

*Legislation is being proposed to extend availability of these funds from July 15, 1995 until September 30, 1997.

(FIGURE 3)

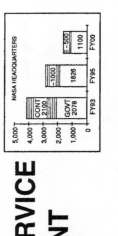

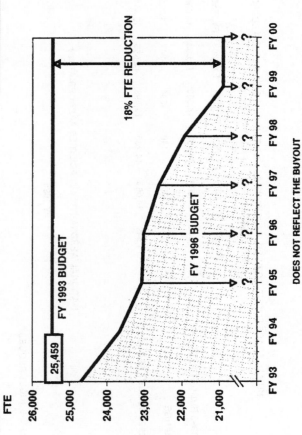

## TOTAL CIVIL SERVICE EMPLOYMENT

NASA HEADQUARTERS

FY 1993 BUDGET

25,459

FY 1996 BUDGET

18% FTE REDUCTION

FTE

DOES NOT REFLECT THE BUYOUT

(FIGURE 4)

25

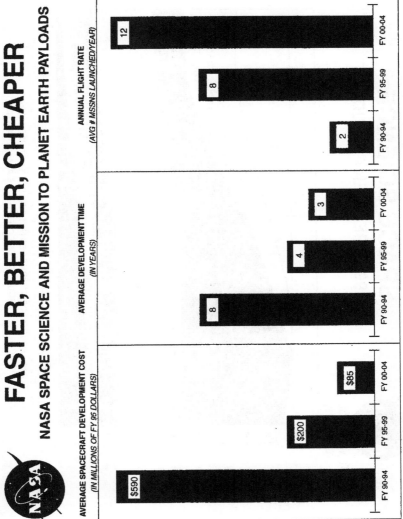

# FASTER, BETTER, CHEAPER

## NASA SPACE SCIENCE AND MISSION TO PLANET EARTH PAYLOADS

**AVERAGE SPACECRAFT DEVELOPMENT COST**
*(IN MILLIONS OF FY 95 DOLLARS)*

**AVERAGE DEVELOPMENT TIME**
*(IN YEARS)*

**ANNUAL FLIGHT RATE**
*(AVG # MSSNS LAUNCHED/YEAR)*

CONSISTENT WITH AN OPERATING SPACE STATION AND A TOTAL AGENCY BUDGET OF ~$13 BILLION

(FIGURE 5)

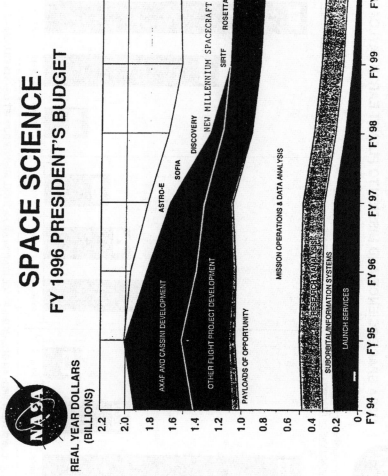

# SPACE SCIENCE
## FY 1996 PRESIDENT'S BUDGET

REAL YEAR DOLLARS
(BILLIONS)

2.2
2.0
1.8
1.6
1.4
1.2
1.0
0.8
0.6
0.4
0.2
0

FY 94   FY 95   FY 96   FY 97   FY 98   FY 99   FY 00

AXAF AND CASSINI DEVELOPMENT

ASTRO-E

SOFIA

DISCOVERY

NEW MILLENNIUM SPACECRAFT

SIRTF

ROSETTA

OTHER FLIGHT PROJECT DEVELOPMENT

PAYLOADS OF OPPORTUNITY

MISSION OPERATIONS & DATA ANALYSIS

RESEARCH ANALYSIS

SUBORBITAL/INFORMATION SYSTEMS

LAUNCH SERVICES

THE ABOVE INFORMATION DOES NOT REFLECT THE UNRESOLVED
PERCENTAGE REDUCTION DIRECTED BY THE ADMINISTRATION

(FIGURE 6)

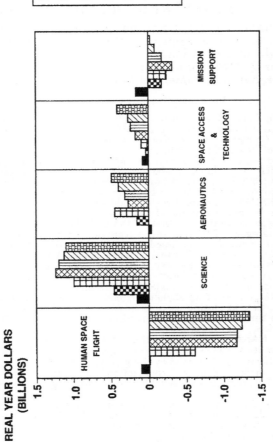

FY 1996 PRESIDENT'S BUDGET
CHANGES FROM FY 1991

REAL YEAR DOLLARS
(BILLIONS)

THE ABOVE INFORMATION DOES NOT REFLECT THE UNRESOLVED
PERCENTAGE REDUCTION DIRECTED BY THE ADMINISTRATION

(FIGURE 7)

Senator BURNS. Mr. Goldin, we know that these are trying times. I thank you for that fine statement.

I notice the chairman of the full committee has joined us this morning. And if he has a statement, I would recognize Senator Pressler at this time. Mr. Chairman, thank you for coming.

## STATEMENT OF SENATOR PRESSLER

The CHAIRMAN. Mr. Chairman, I congratulate you on this hearing. I do have a statement. I shall place it in the record so that we go right into questions.

Senator BURNS. Thank you.

[The prepared statement of Senator Pressler follows:]

PREPARED STATEMENT OF SENATOR PRESSLER

Chairman Burns, I want to thank you for holding this hearing on NASA's FY96 budget request and the commercial space programs at the Departments of Transportation and Commerce. I also want to welcome Dan Goldin and our witnesses from DoT and DoC to our Subcommittee.

As you know, here in Congress, we are struggling to cut spending to reduce the federal deficit and balance the budget. To do this, every federal agency must share the pain. NASA's FY96 budget request clearly reflects its willingness to do just that. Not only is NASA's $14.3 billion budget request less than the current year's spending level, NASA's projected five-year budget calls for a total of $5 billion in cuts.

Achieving budget reductions of that magnitude will be difficult. In fact, that difficulty is reflected in the fact that, of the $5 billion in cuts, $1.9 billion are lumped under the category of "unresolved percentage reduction." To me, that term means that NASA has not yet determined precisely where the cuts will come from.

One matter is certain. Marginal changes at NASA will not save $5 billion. NASA needs to totally rethink the way it has been doing business. To that end, NASA needs to give serious consideration to all reasonable proposals. I know that NASA is doing what it can. For example, I understand that NASA is looking to buyout—or layoff—18 percent of its 23,000-person workforce. It has also been reported that NASA may look at closing or consolidating some of its 12 field centers, many of which have turned into independent bloated bureaucracies. These steps are in the right direction.

However, NASA should not stop there. NASA needs to take a serious look at some other possibilities. For example, many argue that some of NASA's activities may be more cost-effectively performed by the private sector. In this regard, the Space Shuttle is often mentioned as a "privatization" candidate. A private contractor would take over the program and sell Shuttle flights to government and private sector users.

We also need to accept the difficult reality that programs may have to be cut. The $5 billion budget cut assumes that the cost of NASA's programs will remain stable. Historically, however, virtually every NASA program has suffered from massive overruns over its life. In that regard, Space Station has been particularly problematic.

I am a longstanding supporter of Space Station. If Space Station is a success, it will be good news for the science community and for our Nation. Nevertheless, Space Station's checkered past of ballooning costs, schedule delays, and annual redesigns cannot be ignored. Frankly, I am hopeful that the program has finally stabilized to the point where NASA can finally start "cutting metal" instead of redrafting blueprints. However, if the program costs continue upward, Space Station will not fit under NASA's outyear funding profile. At some future date, we may well have to decide between cutting Space Station or some other program. Right now, I remain optimistic, but the Committee will be carefully scrutinizing the program in the meantime.

I am pleased that the budget request includes $1.3 billion for NASA's Mission to Planet Earth. This program will dramatically increase our understanding of the global climate changes that constantly affect our lives. Every week, global change satellites will generate the data equivalent of the entire Library of Congress. Quite literally, NASA will have more data that it knows what to do with.

As Administrator Goldin is aware, several institutions in South Dakota and other Plains States have developed some fascinating ideas on how to use the global climate data, and, more important, how to make that data more useful to the broader community. Their concept is to take the climate data collected at the EROS Data Center in Sioux Falls and then distribute it to farmers, college researchers, teachers, students, and land-use planners in a five-state region. The potential for this concept is limitless, and I will be following its progress with great interest.

Finally, I am eager to hear from our second panel, which will focus on the commercial space industry. In 1992, I cosponsored the Land Remote Sensing Act to give focus and direction to our Landsat program, as well as authorize new private remote sensing ventures. Today, Landsat is a self-sustaining commercial enterprise and at least three U.S. companies have been granted permission to offer competing systems. Globally, land remote sensing is now a $700 million market, which is expected to grow to $30 billion in the next decade. I look forward to hearing from our witnesses about this new market and about the national security problems posed by some of the higher resolution systems of other countries.

Let me again thank Chairman Burns for holding this hearing and welcome our distinguished group of witnesses to our Subcommittee.

Senator BURNS. The 5-year plan, Mr. Goldin, calls for reducing the annual funding from $14.3 billion in fiscal year 1996 to $13.2 billion in fiscal year 2000.

Now, this is $18 billion less than the 5-year profile assumed in the fiscal budget of 1994, and, of course, $5 billion less than the profile assumed in your 1995 budget request.

For some folks and politicians on the Hill, this is Draconian, a Draconian cut. I am wondering how can NASA achieve those kind of cuts and still continue the programs that we have on the drawing boards?

Mr. GOLDIN. Mr. Chairman, I cannot give you the answer for sure, because we are studying it now, but let me tell you the issues. NASA was formed in the late 1950's. At that time, we did not have modern wide-band, multimedia-distributed information and communication systems. Each NASA center was set up to be a self-contained entity, and as a result, we have a tremendous duplication of administrative and management activities. We have overlapped in terms of what centers do. We have multiple centers building the same type of thing. This has to be changed to go to a new system.

The NASA infrastructure was set up in the late eighties and early nineties, when NASA thought that its budget at the end of the decade would be $25 billion.

Our budget at the end of the decade is going to be 40 or 50 percent less than that. So we are going to have to downsize the number of NASA employees.

This is very difficult, because it is unheard of in the Federal Government to do this. But we will have to downsize the number of NASA employees, and along with that, a lot of support services. We want to take the emphasis off support and onto R&D.

And finally, NASA got us into the position of having the government get between the hardware and the contractors. We got NASA managers, thousands of them, managing a multiplicity of contracts where the contractors were not accountable.

We proved on the space station redesign that if we go to industry and give them an objective contract and say you launch the system on thus and such date, and we get out of the way, we are able to eliminate 5,000 jobs on the space station.

We now have built the confidence that if we give industry a higher level of integration, we can make much more progress and save a lot of money.

In fact, we have two studies on the space shuttle, and one was from outside of NASA and one was inside NASA, and on that study we were told that if the contractors came to us and said if we could select a single prime contractor and then perhaps ultimately even privatize that shuttle, we will save money and have a safer system.

Now, I want to tell you, I cannot guarantee safety. If you want to guarantee safety, we should get out of the space business and exploration. But what I can guarantee you is we will be very frugal in making our decisions.

We have an open system where anyone who has a problem could stop the launch of a shuttle. We want to be very careful on how we make decisions, but the one thing I cannot commit is 100 percent safety.

America has to be ready to go to the edge and take risks. We fly in modern jet planes today because of those brave test pilots of the fifties and sixties. And when they had a problem or had a crash, we celebrate their life, and we fly the next day. So we are going to be concerned about safety procedurally, but we cannot guarantee a 100 percent assurance policy.

Senator BURNS. When I hear you say that we are redundant in some of our management practices, and, of course, with each one of the facilities falling under that sort of a management structure, that sounds to me like that is more people than it is facility.

And I am not real sure if people, just the scale back in the number of employees that you might have is really going to attain the cuts or the goals in cuts that you might want.

It sounds to me like we may—I am one of those kind of people who say, "Yes, I am willing to accept a certain amount of risk," as we all do at anytime that we go into an unknown, but I would say that this just is not people alone to attain these cuts.

In other words, something else has to be on the board so that we can get to our goals.

Mr. GOLDIN. Let me say that there will be facilities that are going to be shutdown, and we have a number of facilities that are on the books right now undergoing evaluations. We are going to have to close some buildings and padlock them, and walk away from facilities that we had built, if they are redundant or they do not add significantly to where we are going, or if it costs more doing it in facility "X" versus facility "Y." So I want to emphasize, this is not just people, this is facilities. I also want to say that we are talking about tens of thousands of people. It is not a small number. We do not have the number, but I want you to understand that we are talking about a lot of human beings.

Senator BURNS. Let us switch now to something that I was sort of familiar with. I will ask you these in the second round. I see my yellow light is on here, because everybody is so pushed to attend more than one hearing this morning, but I want to go into more discussion.

I think the American people, the American taxpayers need some information, as much information as we could supply them on the space station, and our relationship with the Russians, and what our plans are.

So at this time I recognize Senator Hutchison, and she has some questions, because I understand that we are all under time constraints as far as attending hearings this morning.

Senator HUTCHISON. Thank you very much, Mr. Chairman. I certainly appreciate that.

Mr. Goldin, many people are concerned about the political and economic situation in Russia, and that they perhaps might not be reliable partners with the space station.

One of the reasons that I think everyone is committed to the space station, or at least the majority in Congress are, is because we do have an international contract. The Congress wants to be a good business partners, but there is that consideration.

Are you optimistic about the partnership with Russia, and are they maintaining their end of the deal to your satisfaction?

Mr. GOLDIN. I can say this, I do not want to say I am optimistic, because we have a country that almost over night attempted to go from totalitarianism to democracy, and from a controlled economy to capitalism, and this is going to take time.

What I can say, and as a NASA administrator, I cannot control the international political scene, but what I can say is the Russians are turning out to be one of our most reliable partners, sitting here today and looking over the arrangement. They deliver hardware, and it is quality hardware. I just asked General Thomas Stafford to go to Russia with a committee, to take a look and give me some confidence that the hardware is quality, that they're meeting all their commitments—he just got back from Russia—because I did not want us to go launch any U.S. astronaut in Russian equipment unless we had that confidence. He is going to prepare a report. He told me he believed that that was a safe possibility. However, we have an obligation to the American people that should something go wrong in Russia, we have alternate contingency plans. And Mr. Sensenbrenner, who is chairman of our subcommittee in the House, had asked us to come up with a program where Russia would be off the critical path, in the event there is such a problem, because the American people want that space station, but they want us to meet our commitment. So we do have contingency plans that we have put together, and we have done appropriate tasks to assure that the space station will be put into orbit.

I will say, however, that we have continuing communications with the Russians. They are going through a very difficult budget crisis, but it appears that space is going to be funded appropriately.

I also want to say there is a tremendous partnership—I got a call last night from the head of the Canadian Space Agency, because the Canadians had another budget cut. The world is trying to deal with this budget crisis. My Canadian partner said, "Dan, we are going to still be able to meet our commitments on the space station."

So there is a camaraderie that is building between the Nations, but we recognize a responsibility and there always will be a risk with the Russians. But by working with them, I think we are building bridges and trying to push them toward democracy. But we will be prepared to launch a space station if they have problems.

Senator HUTCHISON. Thank you. I think that space is a priority in Canada. Hopefully, we will have the same priority and look at the big picture. I sensed, when I was in Russia last year, that it certainly was their priority.

It is something that they have done well, and I am sure they would point out that in the situation with the Mir, it was our ship that was leaking, not theirs.

Mr. GOLDIN. That is correct. It took courage on their part to allow us to dock, but this was a sign that they trust us, and they listened to our engineering analysis. That would not have happened 5 years ago.

Senator HUTCHISON. I thought it was a great coming together in every way, literally as well as figuratively.

Let me say that obviously safety concerns come into the picture when we are in a budget-cutting mode. In my past association with the aviation community, that was the case. It was always a question, is safety going to be first.

Do you feel that we are putting safety concerns at the forefront, and that the budget cuts are going to have an impact on safety?

Mr. GOLDIN. Let me say this. I am continually concerned about safety, and I did not know what safety meant until I became the NASA administrator. I recognize the huge weight on every single person that operates a human space flight system. I went down to NASA–Kennedy just a month or so ago, and because of the safety cuts, I told the people down there safety is the No. 1, two, and three priority at NASA, and if any employee has a concern about safety, I want them to feel comfortable to come forward. I asked that we have a NASA panel and an outside panel look at this, so we could make the right decisions.

I asked our people not to take precipitous steps, and, in fact, I have asked the chief of staff of NASA to set up a very formal appeal process that should be in place with in a week or so, whereby whenever we make any decision on budget, that if someone has a problem relative to safety, they could come into the appeal process and let it be known. We also have a hot line set up.

Saying all this, people should not hide behind safety, apparent safety, to protect budgets. We are doing a lot of things that do not make sense.

Right now we have three contracts for the space shuttle main engines, even though there is one contractor, and we have paperwork flowing, because there are three NASA centers, each of whom have got to own that engine. We are not hurting safety by eliminating those three contracts going to one and putting one person in charge. But there will always be the concern about this.

So I will say we are trying to be prudent. We are going to do the right things. The people have the right spirit, and we will try to deliver.

But the point I want to make is, you could never guarantee safety 100 percent, but you could be conscious about it and make the right decisions.

Senator HUTCHISON. Following the lead of my Chairman, the yellow light came on, which has now turned red, I will give it back to you anyway. Thank you.

Senator BURNS. Senator Pressler.

The CHAIRMAN. Thank you very much, Chairman Burns.

Thank you, Mr. Goldin, for your good testimony.

What is the current status of Mission to Planet Earth? What is the projected total cost of that program, and is the program still designed to generate a 15-year stream of global climate data, and what are the four most important climate phenomena that the current program will look at? You have covered some of this, I know, but——

Mr. GOLDIN. Let me say the following, Mission to Planet Earth is a crucial down payment on protecting the lives and enhancing the economy for future generations.

We have an obligation to understand our climate, the weather patterns, how the human specie is impacting that, and how natural causes are impacting that, just the simple things for insurance companies to understand whether the oceans are going to rise and damage coastal properties, but there are broader issues than that. So at NASA we are committed to it.

We are on track. We are building the ADEOS AM platform, and we are proceeding with the other platform. The budget through the end of this decade is $7.2 billion, and we will only reduce the budget if we could equal or better the performance that we get.

Right now we are exploring possibilities, but more important than that, we believe at the turn of the century we could try some revolutionary new approaches that will give us more results, enable remote sensing industry in America that make it take it from $1 billion a year to perhaps as much as $8 billion a year, by looking at smaller individual spacecraft, perhaps where we would make data buys. But this is something out in the future. We believe we will have a constant stream of data for the next 15 or 20 years. We would like to be able to have a predicted weather model to understand how the weather patterns are changing so farmers could decide whether or not to plant crops a year in advance, because there may be a drought in the geographic area. This is very, very important.

We are going to try to understand how we are impacting the greenhouse gases in the environment. Does it have any effect? We do not know. It may have no effect. But we have to have data on that. So those are the things we are considering, and those are the directions that we are going in. We are committed to future generations on Mission to Planet Earth, and we are not going to back off.

The CHAIRMAN. Now, does NASA have any plans to do anything with radar satellites as part of the Mission to Planet Earth or NASA's space science or exploration programs?

What are the more promising applications of radar satellite, and do you agree that radar satellite data would enhance the usefulness of our LANDSAT data to farmers, researchers, and other users?

Mr. GOLDIN. Radar satellites will also help prospectors for new mineral resources on this planet and perhaps other planets. We have made passive measurements, that is, just looking at reflected light from the sun off the planet Earth with sensors.

We believe we have to go to active sensors, and, in fact, we made two very major measurements with the space radar lab that has given us unbelievable insight into land use and into the environment.

34

We have the National Academy doing a study for us right now to see where we ought to go with the future of these radar satellites, and under the New Millennium program, which we intend to start in the fiscal 1996 budget, we are looking at, instead of multi-billion dollar radar satellites, to see if we could make small radar satellites and fly them in formation to get even more stunning results. So we believe radar is in our future. And by the way, we are looking at cooperative activities with other agencies of the U.S. Government, who are also interested in such radar measurements.

The CHAIRMAN. Now, EOSDIS, the data collection component of Mission to Planet Earth, probably represents the biggest challenge in the program.

Are you confident that EOSDIS will be able to handle the enormous amounts of data the climate change satellites will generate?

Do you want to say anything about those climate change satellites, and when they might be launched, and how they will work? What will be the main type of data collected by EOSDIS, and what will it be used for?

Mr. GOLDIN. I would like to turn that over to Dr. Cordova.

Dr. CORDOVA. All of the data taken from the EOS spacecraft will be put into EOSDIS. Right now there is a version zero of this that takes all the data that has been collected by Mission to Planet Earth. Dr. Kennel can add to my remarks. He is the associate administrator for Mission to Planet Earth. These data will be used by many, many different kinds of people, by scientists, of course, by commerce and industries, by farmers, by many people that are interested in the U.S. natural resources.

The EOSDIS is a large program. Right now we have a number of data analysis and archive centers around the country which have different focuses for these data, to distribute it.

Now, Dr. Kennel, would you like to add to——

Dr. KENNEL. Yes. I would just like to add that NASA is not usually known as an innovator in information technology, but in the case of EOSDIS, it is.

The reason is that the issues associated with integrated environmental and global studies forced us to make an information system that would connect up the various sciences, the sciences of the land, the sciences of the atmosphere, of the ocean, and put all the data immediately on a system that would distribute large amounts of data to the various scientists so that they could work in an interdisciplinary fashion.

It was this requirement that drove the initial development of the EOSDIS system. Then it became absolutely clear that there were a lot of other people who would be interested in this particular and diverse culmination of data, and so now we are working very hard to reach out to the next collection of users, who will be in the commercial and civil arena.

We will have a workshop in June to reach out to those under the principle that the user should design their interface with the system. So I believe that the EOSDIS system will be able to deliver large quantities of data, and the products that the scientists generate, their models, the algorithms, the information at higher levels.

We will all be on this system, and it ultimately will be the way the country—it is the system the country will use to think about earth science.

The CHAIRMAN. Mr. Chairman, could I ask one or two more questions, and then I will——

Senator BURNS. Yes.

The CHAIRMAN. Now, how does the current program of the Mission to Planet Earth proposal compare in cost, content, schedule, and launch plans with the original plans? What have you changed?

Dr. KENNEL. Well, in this——

Mr. GOLDIN. Charlie, could I just——

Dr. KENNEL. Sure.

Mr. GOLDIN [continuing]. Take the first part? The original plan, I believe, was unrealistic. I want to tell you, I was in industry at the time, and I was very vocal about that. We were attempting to put six 40,000-pound satellites, which cost multi billions of dollars, with too many sensors, into orbit. And on paper, the original EOS constellations look good, but I am not sure that we could have achieved that objective.

So what we have done is we have downsized the program in this decade from $18 billion to about $7.2 billion. We took the size of the satellites down from 40,000 pounds. We have some satellites that are 10,000 pounds, other satellites that are hundreds of pounds. And in the process, I believe, we have a very realistic set of data that will make a major contribution to the future.

So by comparing the two programs, it is very hard to say what could have happened, but I was concerned, and many in the community were concerned that if you put too many sensors in one spacecraft, what would you do if you failed one sensor? Would you launch another multi-billion dollar 40,000-pound satellite?

So there is some very significant issues associated with it. But that is an overview. I would like Dr. Kennel to make a few comments.

Dr. KENNEL. The only comment I would like to make is the program went from $17 billion to the year 2000, when it was first proposed, to the current $7.25 billion. This is just the opposite direction from which the SSC went. It is going in the opposite direction. I think we have the costs now at a much more firmer shape. The other point is that we did not slip a launch. We advanced launches, we advanced content into the earlier time period. So I suspect that the new program is a strong program.

For the last three looks that we have had at the program, the number of instruments has remained, with the exception of one, the same, which is a statement that the scientists have held on to their original vision, and under the stress of the budgets and other things, we evolved the technology toward smaller and more diverse spacecraft, and we evolved our system toward a greater international collaboration in some of the smaller parts of the program.

The CHAIRMAN. I have one final question. I have some additional questions for the record. If you were to talk to a taxpayer, which I am sure you do every day, and you all are taxpayers, how would you justify the Mission to Planet Earth, if some hard-nosed taxpayer said, "I want a dollar-for-dollar"—what are we going to get out of this?

Are we going to get as much out of this as we put into it? Do we have any cost benefit projections or any analyses of what the businessmen and the taxpayers of America get out of the Mission to Planet Earth, and are we going to get a dollar back for every dollar we put in, or more?

Mr. GOLDIN. Let me answer it this way, there is not one T.V. news program or radio program that does not rely completely on the weather satellites developed by NASA in prior years, but we made a very limited set of measurements.

But in Mission to Planet Earth, we are going to make many more robust measurements that is going to touch everybody's life.

There are decisions that this U.S. Congress is going to have to make in the years ahead about our environment. And you do not want to make decisions based upon passionate emotion. You want good, hard scientific facts, because they are decisions that could impact the economy. It could touch everybody's life in the world, and these decisions are going to have to be made.

Second, it would be irresponsible for future generations if we have the capacity to do predictive weather modeling that could give us near- and long-term weather modeling for natural disasters, to understand the level of the ocean, to understand and help farmers plant by the yard, so they know how to lay down fertilizer, and they know how to water.

We are working with the wine growers, Robert Mondavi, in California, on how to protect the vines against the devastation from valoxeri.

This is probably one of the most important programs ever undertaken by the Federal Government. This is exactly what the Federal Government ought to be doing, but what we have to assure is that NASA does not get into the political business. We perform this in true scientific fashion, and leave the politics for people who are outside the NASA domain.

The CHAIRMAN. Mr. Chairman, if you would indulge me for one more question. This is absolutely my last. I promise.

I understand that later this year NASA plans a review of the nine data centers to be used in Mission to Planet Earth. What criteria will be used in evaluating the data centers, and what do you think the results will be?

Mr. GOLDIN. We have an obligation to the American people to allow Darwin to rule, and this is survival of the fittest in a down budget.

We have to make sure, and I will use the Chairman's words, that what we are doing is relevant to the American people, and not relevant to the people working in these data acquisition centers.

We want to make sure we meet the promise that we will be able to get predictive models of weather. We want to make sure we will meet the promise that every single American will be able to get this data, real-time, off the Internet.

We have an obligation to do that, so our criteria is not dollars in, not jobs in, but will this touch the American people, just in the question that you asked us, will it impact the lives of future generations, and is the data meaningful.

And we are going to have a scientific panel, we will have a peer review process, and we will make sure that it is an objective one, and we will make sure that the Congress understands the rules up front, so that you could talk to your constituents and say NASA did the right thing.

Dr. KENNEL. Let me just add, I know you have a particular concern for a center in South Dakota, and it is our only land DAC. It has a particular responsibility for watching after data that is concerned with land use, that this is an area of concern that has grown in the last 5 years, since the program started.

And so I would—the review will, of course, look at the value of all—the value of the service being performed. We will also be seeking out cooperative arrangements in our data centers.

The CHAIRMAN. Thank you. Mr. Chairman, I must go off to another hearing. I will try to come back, but if I cannot, I ask you now to consent to place the remainder of my questions in the record.

Senator BURNS. Without objection, we will sure do that.

Senator BURNS. I made the announcement at the opening of this hearing that if you have questions, you can submit them to the Director, and he can respond both to you and the Committee.

Mr. GOLDIN. May I just make one more comment to Senator Pressler?

Senator BURNS. Yes.

Mr. GOLDIN. Senator Pressler, I would like to give you an example of the very intricate weather system and environmental system we have on this planet. Through the spacecraft and the astronauts on the shuttle, we have been able to detect a phenomena that goes like this. The winds blow on the Sahara Desert. It lifts the sand into the upper atmosphere.

These sands form a cloud that goes right across the Atlantic Ocean and land on the rain forests in Brazil, where these sands fertilize the rain forests, which cause the trees there to be nourished, which provides the conversion of carbon dioxide into oxygen, which protects the overall climate on this Earth. By understanding what is going on, we could have a better understanding of where we have to protect bio mass on this planet. We all breathe the same air.

This is a process that we got total understanding from by looking down with spacecraft on planet Earth. There are a multiplicity of such phenomena. We understand so little about our own environment that it is crucial that we perform tasks like this.

Senator BURNS. Thank you. I might suggest with that last answer that there are some farmers that are going around and looking for work, and they can answer some of those questions for you. You will not have to put a space shuttle up there. They can understand some of those things.

I want to welcome ranking member Senator Rockefeller to the Committee this morning. I just have a couple of questions that—I liked your explanation on how important the Russian involvement is on the space station, and the actions that we have taken.

As reported in "Aerospace Daily," the Russian situation, there are some people who think that it is on the verge of collapse. There are some fears there that we have programs in place that can take care of or fill that hole, should something happen.

I personally think that that would be devastating to the program, but nonetheless, I congratulate this Administration. I think we were in the same room with Vice President Gore the night that we went through this whole litany with the scientists from Russia, and I would hate to see that happen.

Now we have another situation coming in, as reported today, in the European community, where Germany and France have asked to place a $2 billion cap on their funding of the space station.

That is sort of a concern to me, but Germany is very active in their enthusiasm for this, where France has not taken—their degree of enthusiasm is a little bit less.

Does that concern you whenever we start talking about these programs in which we have joint cooperation?

Mr. GOLDIN. There are two things that get my attention, safety and how our international partners are faring in this world. But we are dealing in a world in transition.

This is a world that is going out from the twentieth century to the twenty-first, going from a manufacturing age to an information age, hopefully going from cold war to peace. There is a lot of readjustment taking place, and for the space-faring Nations to say space has to be outside of any budget cuts will be wrong. So what we have to do is have a sense of teamwork and work with our partners.

The United States cut the costs of the space station, and our European and Japanese partners initially said, well, you cannot do that. And then they said we recognize that there is a budget crisis in the United States, and they were tolerant of us.

So as our European partners go through the very difficult downsizing of government and cutting of budgets, we have to be tolerant of them.

I went to Europe and I told them we applaud the fact that they are trying to downsize, and we want to work with them. And we are not going to stand in judgment, and if they want to do a number of tasks that will cause it to be downsized, if they want to work with us, we will be pleased to work with them.

Last year we had a crisis in Canada. They had a huge budget cut, but they were able to work through it, and I am confident that as partners we will work through it. But we cannot say space is immune from budget cuts, because we have to be part of the solution. If we are going to have a future world where countries work together, we cannot sit in judgment of our partners. We have to support them.

Senator BURNS. Well, I would think that this Chairman, and this Committee, I think, will monitor those activities around the world, because I think they will have some effect on how we approach these programs in space.

I have some more questions to ask, but before I get to mine, I want to recognize the ranking member, and welcome him here this morning. And I see by the clock that he's running just about on time for him. Senator Rockefeller, thank you for coming this morning.

## STATEMENT OF SENATOR ROCKEFELLER, IV

Senator ROCKEFELLER. Thank you, Mr. Chairman.

It is impressive to see how quickly you are moving into this area. I might say this is the first day in the 10 years that I have been in the Senate that I had three committees meeting at exactly the same time.

What they are saying about me in the third committee right now, I do not even dare to think about.

I want to make a couple of points, Dan, and then I will ask you questions. First of all, I believe in you. I think you are a good leader and a good director.

I think that is needed, because with the budget actions that we are about to take, however it comes out, there is going to be cuts. You faced up to that very early. You want to do the right thing for the agency.

You are willing to even take criticism from your own ranks, so long as you feel that you are doing the right thing. I happen to think that you are—streamlining and cost cutting.

There are two things that particularly interest me, the budget constraints that face NASA and us. The Administration told NASA last year to expect essentially level budgets over the next several years, and then in December, the President decided to cut $5 billion out of your budget over the next 5 years.

That is a lot. Of course, everybody is going to be cutting a lot, whether the balanced budget amendment passes or not. There are going to be cuts all over government, because we are all headed in that direction.

The fact that the House has done $35 billion of recision cuts is terrifying, in a sense, because it shows what Congress can do when it wants to. You are not the ones who are asking for the Draconian cuts.

So I would say that to those who work for you, wherever they are in the country, it is not Dan Goldin or your colleagues in NASA who are asking to make these Draconian cuts. It is us. They should understand that, even as they vent their anger at some of their leadership as well as us.

But will those in Congress who support the space program be able to protect the budget? That's the worrisome factor. If major cuts have to be made, where should they be made, at what cost to our space exploration and research?

Will some of our colleagues push for huge cuts in school lunches and Medicare to protect NASA? That's the other side of the equation.

So if you listen, it is nothing but hard times. So let me ask you my question. Chairman Burns and I last year introduced the NASA technology bill. We are very protective of that bill.

We care about that bill. We watch its every motion and wiggle. The idea of that was to help Americans realize that NASA is relevant to the regular United States economy, the non–NASA economy.

Now, I do not want to come out in left field with you on this, but with all that you have going on, and all that you have to worry about, you did, nevertheless, give this Committee assurances that NASA was changing its old ways of doing business to folks on approaches and technologies that benefited both NASA missions and the U.S., as we say, competitiveness.

You had some small NASA industry programs that you began, I believe, last year, and I wonder if there are any results that were beginning to show on any of that, or is there anything that you can tell me about this effort?

Mr. GOLDIN. Let me say in the broader sense, I do not think that we have results right off the bat, but we intend to do one fundamental thing at NASA, we have spent too large a fraction of our budget on operations and support, and too small a fraction on R&D.

With this $5 billion cut, we intend to get NASA as much out of the operations and support business, and more into the advanced R&D as possible.

The other thing we want to do is get to be an enabler for industry, and we are trying to work with—we have an effort going at NASA Stennis, in Mississippi, it's called the Earth Observation Commercial Applications Program, where we are trying to help— we are working with 300 companies to help build a whole new industry in remote sensing that will create opportunity for them, and allow us to understand the environment.

We are going in the direction of getting out of the business of telling contractors how to do things, and we are starting a new launch vehicle program that we hope will start a whole new industry in this country, by asking the contractors to take charge, and if they want to use NASA resources to subcontract with NASA, so that they could determine the market forces. So this is the direction we are going in, and we made tremendous progress.

One of the points I would like to make is very important for the Congress to understand, that is, under the stress of budget cuts, there will always be issues that survive in the present.

I would like to give you two data points. America is No. 9teenth in the world in percentage of dollars spent for corporate R&D, as a percentage of gross national product, nineteenth. All the G7 countries are ahead of us. And in non-defense R&D, America is number twenty-eighth in the world.

So as the Congress takes a look at where we are going, we have to say at some point in time, we must draw the line and say we have to have some investment funds for the future.

So that is an issue that I cannot give you a solution to, but it is an issue that we are all going to have to work on, because you make that investment fund zero, and there will not be a well to dip into 10 years from now when we need that technology.

But I want to assure you, we are not just meeting the spirit of what you said, in terms of this working with industry, we are really doing it.

Senator ROCKEFELLER. Thank you, Mr. Chairman.

Senator BURNS. I was going to give you a little more time, if you wanted it. You can ask one more, if you want. Go ahead.

Senator ROCKEFELLER. Have you talked this morning about the so-called switch to the single-company responsibilities as opposed to the multiple subcontractors? I think that is a very interesting and important concept, and a wise one.

Mr. GOLDIN. I talked a little bit about it, but I would like to expand on it a bit. One of the issues that we have had is NASA proudly would say that we contract ninety percent of our budget, and we have 10 percent of the budget for the NASA employees.

But when we took a look at how we were doing business, we found that NASA, in the broader sense, was not performing objective contracting. We were hiring our contractors to do support services almost on a time and materials basis.

So if you are a contractor, you are not bad, your objective is to get as many people in, because that is how you earn your money, and no one is really accountable.

So as a fundamental rule as part of this restructuring, we are saying we want to raise the contractors to a much higher level and give them prime end item responsibility and give them objective contracts, and in the limit, get NASA out of the business of managing a whole host of contracts, having a number of support contractors to help them manage it, and go to industry with objective contracts.

We have recommendations from the Chris Kraft panel which says we could save a significant fraction of the shuttle budget and improve the safety if we go to a single prime contractor, instead of having thousands of NASA employees, and an even larger number of support contractors managing 50 contracts. We are going to apply that concept across the board.

Senator ROCKEFELLER. Thank you.

Senator BURNS. Into an another area, Mr. Director, we have heard a great deal about the new Millennium, and some programs that ave been developed in the past couple of years or so regarding that.

Since 1964, NASA has spent $236 million on a project called Gravity Probe B. Its stated purpose was to, I think, test Einstein's theory of relativity.

According to published reports, the scientific community has serious doubts about the viability of that, the scientific viability, that is, and although the program has undergone at least 17 studies over the years to evaluate its merit, NASA has commissioned it for one more study.

If the latest National Academy of Sciences study does not find Gravity Probe B to be a national priority, what do you think the possibilities of further funding in that program would be?

Mr. GOLDIN. Zero.

Senator BURNS. Could we also say the same thing about the Alpha, the Alpha's U.S. laboratory module currently for launch for November, 1988?

And when we talk about Alpha, what I would say is, are we now starting to design—well, this space station, and then the laboratories, are we now, if we are going to the corporate level, have we started making plans for that launch?

And when it finally becomes a reality in 1998 in space, have we already started the work on special projects that will go on-line immediately when it gets into space?

Mr. GOLDIN. Let me turn that over to Dr. Cordova, because I would like to give you more than a one-word answer for Gravity Probe B, because I think that would be inappropriate.

There have been a number of studies, but you have to understand, Gravity Probe B has been around for a number of years. I was one of the major supporters of it.

And for the last 3 years, I put it in the budget, because I felt we needed to do exciting science. But in the last half year, a number of members of the National Academy came to visit me and said they saw three problems with that program.

They feel that it might have been overtaken by events, not that it was a bad program, but there had been other scientific findings that have caused the results for Gravity Probe B to perhaps not be valid. Some of them said that the accuracy that Gravity Probe B had on a phenomena called lens tearing may not be accurate enough to do really significant science, and third, their concern was that they may not be able to guarantee the accuracy of one part in a hundred on that.

So rather than being the judge and the jury, I felt we needed to go to the National Academy, go to the members who had been concerned and say, "Look, we are in a new world."

You are going to have to help the government make decisions, and you cannot come in and complain, and then judge what we say. You have to be part of the decision process.

So I sent them a set of criteria, and I asked them to get the best scientists and engineers we had in the country, people who were not going to be involved, so we would get comparison of program A to program B, to make some hard decisions.

And I feel this is going to be more and more the thing we are going to do, and I come back to the statement I made, Darwin has to rule supreme, and we have to have a peer review process, and if you cannot cut it, we cut your programs. This has to happen. I do not want to sound harsh or cruel, but in good conscious to the American people, if something is overtaken by events, or something is being improperly managed, we cannot have tradition rule and have ten- and twenty-year white collar entitlement programs. We have to cancel those, also.

So I have an open mind on Gravity Probe B, but if the Academy comes back and answers the questions that we asked in a negative manner, I think we have no choice but to cancel it.

Senator BURNS. Well, I would just put a footnote on that, because I think any time that you go into any scientific research or anything like that, into the unknown, we do not know what was in there, and had we not done it, then those questions would still be relative today. But I would just say I think that the Darwin theory that you have adopted is very apropos.

Let us go into another area where I think—no. Dr. Cordova, I will let you comment on Alpha, and what is being done now to make sure that we have—the laboratory is going to be—what will be demanded of people who will use it, and those contacts being made now, plans for 1998?

Dr. CORDOVA. Yes. We have a process by which we are involving the science community, our international partners, the space station offices, all the relevant crews have formulated a schedule for bringing together their plans for the utilization of this station.

Sometime this year MOUs will be signed with our international partners, and each of those partners will bring—once the MOUs are signed, then they will be constructing their own plans for the utilization, depending on the amount of resources that they have. We have already started on our plan.

Right now we have about 400 life and microgravity science investigators. By the year 2000, we will have some 900 just in this country alone.

We have, as you know, six major facilities that we are developing for this station. By the year 2002, all those facilities will be completely installed on the station.

But way before that, individual facilities will be—a particular rack or an early part of that facility will be installed to ensure that users will be able to use it and test that before the second rack, and the whole facility is completed.

Those facilities span the whole gamut, from the major centrifuge facility, which is the biggest piece to the gravitation biology facility, a human research facility, furnace facility, biotechnology, and a fluids and combustion facility.

We do, of course, work very closely with the scientific community on this, and they are satisfied, from looking at current plans.

And we have had a number of proposals, opportunities for them to propose investigations for earlier missions to the space station, like the Mir mission, and free-flyers, and so forth, to get ready for the station, that they feel confident with the plan that we set out and also with the budget that we have, that they are going to be able to do very good science on the station.

Senator BURNS. Is there anybody wanting to put any money up front to help us build this thing, so they can carry on with their scientific research?

Dr. CORDOVA. Are you asking scientists to put up the money to——

Senator BURNS. Yes. [Laughter.]

Senator BURNS. Well, no, but I mean the private sector, I think, will eventually be involved in this. Although, we sort of grin about that, but I think it would behoove us to look into that possibility.

Mr. GOLDIN. Let me say this, that the chairman of Space Hab has approached us, and they are considering some investments.

They would like to see us privatize or commercialize the operation of the space station after construction is complete, and we are considering to do just that.

And we have a clause in the contract that says 1 year after the construction is complete, we are going to recompete the operations and logistics of that space station.

And we are planning right now today, by starting the process of bringing in corporations—until the laboratory is complete, you cannot do it, but we would love to privatize the operation of that space station, and a number of corporations indicated an interest, but not a commitment, yet. We want to do that.

Senator BURNS. Senator Rockefeller.

Senator ROCKEFELLER. Do you have that "Aerospace Daily" clipping? I like the privatization, because I think, again, looking at budget realities for the future, there just going to be more and more of this kind of thing.

I do not know if I am in the position to scientifically defend that at this point, but the concept of getting something going, particularly as you move to prime contractors, where certain people focus on getting something done, and then moving to privatize, seems to me to make great sense.

I just glanced at this, and then I tossed it aside, and then I said, "Well, no, maybe I better bring it up after all."

What our Chairman indicated here, that there will be a number of space programs that might be cut out on the Russian side in the next year, 2 years, or 3 years, and that leads to a question: To what extent that does jeopardize what is going on with Russia. And then also the fact that on the European side, which was going to be my second question, I see here now that they have not been convinced on a station, an official concedes. And you think of the Japanese, and then you pretty much run the gamut with those who can do it.

Maybe you have already answered this, but I have not heard it: Does one just get these things and truck forward, since we have no choice anyway, and since we cannot really predict what is going to happen, or do we have no choice but to commit to work with the Russians, one, because that was the agreement that the Vice President set out—and I think we would agree with it—and second, you cannot tell because it could be weak today and strong tomorrow, you simply cannot tell? Do we just truck ahead?

Mr. GOLDIN. Let me——

Senator ROCKEFELLER. And why are Europeans so sure? I mean the Italians are in on this. The Canadians are in on this. The Japanese are in on this in ways on the space station. They are all part of it. Why are they so wary about all of this?

Mr. GOLDIN. Well, let me take you in a time machine to the summer of 1993, when the Japanese, the Europeans and the Canadians said, "What in the world is going on in America? You continue to debate the space station, and we continue to move forward."

And there was enormous frustration with America, where we have vote after vote. I think we have had 16 or 17 votes in the almost 3 years that I have been the Administrator of NASA.

And each time before the vote, I will see letters from foreign ministers, heads of agencies, saying, "What's going on in America?" I think the answer to the question is we live in a world with changing times. And if we try and be too sharp in our reaction to things, and we want to just hold shotguns to people's heads and not recognize that there is a change in the air, in going from a manufacturing society to an information society, in the world transitioning from a lot of totalitarian states and trying to get to democracy, with a society where you have people that were in pretty primitive conditions coming up to an industrial condition, we have got to have a flexibility, if we want to have a world, and we are going into the 21st century without aiming missiles across oceans again.

And we have to look at our international relationships as true partners. The Canadians had a terrible problem last year. And I will never forget the call I got from Roland Duret, the head of the Canadian Space Agency. He told me, "Canada has an unbelievable budget crisis, and the Canadian budget is going to be cut." He did not even know if they would have a space agency. And the first thing I said is, "Roland, we are going to work with you." We are going to see how we can achieve the objective of building a research station in earth orbit that will benefit humanity. We know how to build weapons. We have proved that. We know how to aim weapons. We have proved that. But we have not proved it in a major technology project on an international basis that we could do things to benefit humankind.

We are going to have a lot of bumps in the road. You cannot have a weak stomach with this. And the Europeans are going through an enormous financial crisis. It does not mean that they do not support the space station, but we are going to have to work with them.

They have some concepts and ideas where they want to be able to have their ability to participate in the logistics, not just the building of it, and they want to use their Ariane–5 vehicle.

There are things we could do to work with them. I believe we will get over this crisis, but we will have another crisis next year and one the year after. The key thing is: Where does America stand? And do we have the stomach to maintain commitments that we make?

Senator ROCKEFELLER. Yes. I think I agree with that, and I think that is a very wise answer. And I am not trying to make you look so good, Dan, but I do agree with that.

And it occurs to me, Taiwan, which is now the sixth largest economy in the world, has no aerospace program of its own. I am talking aviation, not——

Mr. GOLDIN. It does. When I was in industry, I helped them get started in the space business. They have a space program.

Senator ROCKEFELLER. All right. But they do not have an aviation.

Mr. GOLDIN. Oh, yes, sir.

Senator ROCKEFELLER. They have airlines——

Mr. GOLDIN. Yes, sir.

Senator ROCKEFELLER [continuing]. That have purchased, but they do not make. They do not manufacturer. They tried to buy McDonnell Douglas, as you remember. They tried to buy British Airways, and it did not work.

We went at them. We, in West Virginia, went at them with the idea of a facility. We had a terrific inventor in Texas, by the name of Ed Swearingem, whose name you probably know, who did the Lear Jet and Aerobus and Jet Star and other things.

They had come up with a configuration of a new corporate jet, and there has not really been a new corporate jet in a generation, if you think about it.

And it is beginning to pay the price citations coming out with something that is relatively new. And we convinced them, and Ed convinced them, that they should start their own. You know, why buy the British or try to buy ours, but do their own.

They have the money. They have more money on the table than any country in the world from their current account surplus. So, in other words, and now that they have agreed to it, we are going to do it. It is going ahead. It is going to be started in West Virginia, and it will be carried on in Taiwan.

So, as you say, you cannot tell what will happen from 1 year to the next. And I think your philosophy is right. You just have to keep trucking.

Mr. GOLDIN. It is risky, but I think we have no choice but to be in the world and make sure America is in a leadership position.

Senator ROCKEFELLER. Yes.

Mr. GOLDIN. Leadership is different than control and management. Leadership says you have the best technology, the best management strengths, and people will come with you. And that is a lot different than directing people.

Senator ROCKEFELLER. Yes. I think the main thing, Mr. Chairman—and then I will stop, and I know I have to go—is that my message would be to NASA employees, and there are many of them, what I said before, and that is these budget cuts are not your idea.

They are the President's idea, Conrad's idea, Jay's idea. In other words, we are imposing these things on you. You have to respond to them in a way which keeps the program going.

And you cannot possibly do that looking at the future and looking at the situation without making very, very hard choices. And your people need to know that.

Mr. GOLDIN. Thank you.

Senator BURNS. Mr. Goldin, just a couple of other areas that I will ask you about.

And I thank Senator Rockefeller for coming this morning and adding his insight to this.

Infrastructure and our commitment to civilian aircraft: As a result of that, and of course your withdrawal of the $400 million, as far as the air tunnels are concerned, I think we need to talk about that a little more.

Does that show a lack of commitment to civilian aircraft of aeronautics, or can we expect that that infrastructure will be part of NASA and our commitment to this country's ability to compete in this area?

Mr. GOLDIN. Let me first say, before I turn it over to Dr. Huntress, who is in charge of the aeronautics group—Harris, I am sorry. I have been here awhile, sitting.

Look, I think there may be some confusion. The OMB recommendation in our 1996 budget request is not to eliminate the $400 million. We said we wanted a further decision on a year or two downstream, and we put some wording in to get statutory language which will allow us to retain that $400 million, but just not add another. Now, the $400 million is budget authority, not outlay authority. And the administration opposes the recision in the House of that $400 million. We support the retention of the $400 million in the budget. We have the money in outlays above and beyond that to do all the studies, to do the pre-site selection, and to really understand and work with the industries to see how much this is going to cost. One of the things we do not want to do to America is to make a quick judgment on how much it is going to cost, come forward for the funding, get industry to put in money, and come back and say, "Oh, we are so sorry. It is going to overrun." So we want to collect the data, and that is going to take a year or two. Industry is sending some of their finest people.

Instead of having NASA do the study, we are giving a contract to an industrial consortium led by the Boeing Company with

McDonnell Douglas, Pratt–Whitney, GE, Northrop and Lockheed. So we are going to have industry come back and tell us that.

The second issue here is: America has built only one new wind tunnel since the forties and fifties. Europe has built six. We have got to understand what to do. And we want to have a different partnership, instead of keep coming back to the America people and say, "We want to have a government project." We do not want that. The industry is having very difficult times right now, and the industry is experiencing a downturn in orders. We wanted to also give the industry a year or two to see when this recovery would come, so they might be able to make a larger contribution.

They have already committed to put in hundreds of millions of dollars, and we would like to give them some time to put in a little bit more so the American people will know that this is really different.

So we support the retention of that $400 million. All we want to do is defer the decision so we do not have to come back here again with sad faces. We want to do the right thing for America.

Senator BURNS. Dr. Harris, do you want to comment on that or on the development of wind tunnels?

I have, also, with our—I guess my other question is on our commercial centers for development of space and our technology transfer centers. I think that is a discussion that we can have at another time, but I still think they are very important, as far as NASA's outreach is concerned.

I have a question from Senator Lott, however, that I would submit at this time. Several years ago, the Advanced Solid Rocket Motor, ASRM Program, was canceled after a considerable amount of taxpayer money was invested in constructing the state-of-the-art facilities at Yellow Creek, Mississippi.

In order that the taxpayers' investment not go to waste, plans were made to move nozzle production activities from Utah to the Yellow Creek facility. I understand that the soon-to-be-released Inspector General's report is critical of the transfer of nozzle activities.

What are the principal findings, and what will the impact be, will the report have on the plans to transfer the nozzle work to Yellow Creek? "Creek," I guess they say here. [Laughter.]

Mr. GOLDIN. In the South Bronx, we say "crick."

Senator BURNS. Do you? [Laughter.]

Mr. GOLDIN. This is a very difficult situation. The Inspector General's report has come out. And the Inspector General's report recommended that we not transfer the nozzle activity from Utah to Yellow Creek, because they felt it would add an additional $800 million over the life cycle of the Shuttle Program. Now, we at NASA are evaluating that report. And although we may disagree with the absolute number, a number of things have changed since then.

When we talked about assuring the taxpayers that we have made an investment in Yellow Creek, that we take advantage of the facilities there, we intended to put a nozzle center of excellence there that Thiokol would build.

Now this was going to have more than just a space shuttle program. Thiokol was going to build all their solid rocket motor nozzles in Yellow Creek. Since that time, they had no other business, and the only facility that was to go into Yellow Creek was the shuttle business. This is part of the problem. But the other part of the problem is, at the time we did it, we knew it would cost more money, but we were trying to do the right thing to amortize the investment the government already made.

But now, with the budget coming down, you get a $5 billion budget cut, you have to say, "We have to be balanced across the board. And if it costs more money in Yellow Creek, are we doing the right thing for the overall program?"

Now, I have tremendous compassion for the people in Yellow Creek. I went down there and committed to this. I gave my word. I wish I could control the budget in this country.

Now, we have not made a final decision. We have to evaluate what the Inspector General's report said. We have to take a look at all these cuts we made.

But I want to tell you, it has not been a pleasant two or 3 weeks for me, because I have gone to some of our biggest supporters in the Congress and some of our biggest supports in America, and I have had to tell them the budget has been cut.

And we have to be objective, and we may have to shutdown facilities if we cannot say this is the most efficient way of doing it.

And I want to tell you, Senator Lott has been one of the biggest supports of the space program, and the people in Yellow Creek—this is not the first time it happened to them.

TVA was going to put a nuclear reactor there. They got it started and stopped. The ASRM got started and then canceled by the Congress.

And the people in Yellow Creek have got to begin to say, "You know, is this American government for real?" They put up roads and hospitals and schools. This is very painful, but I feel I am responsible, and I have a fiduciary responsibility to the American people.

If the budget gets cut, we have to ask: What is right for the American people? And I hope that we don't cause such problems with our supporters that it will give them great pain. But this is my job. I accepted this job, and I will carry it out.

Senator BURNS. Well, we appreciate your attitude on that, and we want to continue to work together to make NASA as good as it can be and still carry out the programs.

And there again, we have to very, very cautious. One of my priorities, of course, is safety. And I think—even though understanding the risks that we take whenever we start to explore the unknown.

I thank you. We will have some more questions, and you may respond to the Committee and individuals and members on this Committee. We thank you for coming this morning, and that is all the questions I have at this time.

Mr. GOLDIN. Thank you, Mr. Chairman.

Senator BURNS. We have with us this morning, and to hear their testimony, Dr. Keith Calhoun–Senghor, Director of Office of Air and Space Commercialization from the Department of Commerce, and Mr. Frank Weaver, who is Director of Commercial Space Transportation from the Department of Transportation.

We look forward to having their testimony this morning, because as we take space more seriously now, we think there will be applications other than scientific that will involve both the Department of Transportation and the Department of Commerce.

So we look forward to hearing their testimony this morning.

Mr. Calhoun-Senghor, thank you for coming this morning, and we look forward to your testimony. Thank you for coming.

## STATEMENT OF KEITH CALHOUN-SENGHOR, DIRECTOR, OFFICE OF AIR AND SPACE COMMERCIALIZATION, U.S. DEPARTMENT OF COMMERCE

Mr. CALHOUN-SENGHOR. Thank you very much, Mr. Chairman.

It is a pleasure to be here on behalf of Secretary Brown and the Commerce Department, sir.

Senator BURNS. You might want to pull that microphone in to you so that——

Mr. CALHOUN-SENGHOR. Is that better, sir?

Senator BURNS. You bet.

Mr. CALHOUN-SENGHOR. Thank you.

Senator BURNS. I have an auctioneer's voice. So you have to project that out pretty good.

Mr. CALHOUN-SENGHOR. Thank you, sir. I would like to, if it is allowed, to submit my written comments for the record and to simply highlight a few of the points in my written testimony.

I would like to say that this is a very important time to be here. It is very exciting, and we welcome the opportunity to highlight where we are going.

The written testimony we have submitted will deal with some of the details in terms of some of the budget items, but I would like to just touch on a few points that the chairman made during his opening remarks, and also touch on a few of the directions, essentially the four areas that we are going to be focusing on.

By way of background, sir, we are in the Office of the Secretary of Commerce, and we work with the various bureaus and with the private sector in terms of commercial space policies, specifically with NOAA, within the Commerce Department, the International Trade Administration, Bureau of Export Administration, Technology Administration and National Telecommunications and Information Agency.

Our mission is to assist the Secretary in the formulation of policies to promote the commercial space activities of U.S. industry and to promote the competitiveness of the private sector.

Commercial space is an extremely important area now, because, as the chairman knows, this is an emerging area. And it is seen in a number of ways by the emergence of the big LEO systems, the low-earth-orbiting systems, that will play a very important role in the national information infrastructure, as well as the global information infrastructure, and by the emergence of new industries, such as remote sensing, commercial remote sensing, as part of the President's policy, which will play an extremely important role in terms of this new information explosion that we are seeing.

The office, in looking at the trends in terms of where things are going, essentially has four areas it will be focusing on in the upcoming year. The first and most important is remote sensing, commercial remote sensing.

The President's policy of last year essentially unshackled U.S. industry to allow them to compete in an industry that has proven itself to be commercially viable and which currently is dominated by essentially the French and Russians in terms of the provision of commercial remote images.

It is, I think, a recognition of the fact that we are entering a new age, a new era, and that is an information era. Remote sensing is essentially an information technology. It is part of the spectrum of information from voice to data to GPS location data and imagery.

And it is very important that we as a nation remain technologically competitive in that area, because this is one of the areas where there is a direct linkage between our commercial viability and our national security.

Our ability to be commercially viable, to be a major player in this area, will have a direct effect on our ability to protect our national security.

And the President's policy, with the leadership of the Congress in this area, this is one of the areas where the Land Remote Sensing Act, frankly, pushed this, and the policy balances our economic and our national security and is supported by the intelligence community, the Defense Department, Commerce and State Departments.

The important thing is to stay ahead of the problem and to keep us ahead of our competition on this. In many ways, particularly in this area, the race is, for the commercial companies, no longer to the moon; it is to market.

And getting first to market and being able to take space and make it relevant to the average citizen, I think, is the challenge that we face as a government.

The second area that we are dealing with is the national space transportation policy. As you know, the President also last year signed a policy that talked in terms of what we do about our next generation launch vehicles.

And in many ways, it was groundbreaking, because what it did is it explicitly for the first time recognized the importance of the commercial sector in launch policy decisions. It said we have to get them involved.

And Frank Weaver at Transportation worked very closely with the Commerce Department on this.

And what it said is that the Department of Transportation and the Department of Commerce have the mandate to get the private sector more directly involved in joint partnerships with the government in terms of developing next generation launch vehicles that will be relevant to our competitiveness, as well as involving them from the start in terms of our commercial designs, so that we have an industry that has a vehicle at the end of the day that is relevant to them, as well as more cost effective for taxpayers.

The third priority is launch agreements, international launch agreements. We have concluded launch agreements with the Russians. We have initialed a launch agreement with the Chinese. And the Ukrainians, who also have some launch capacity, have expressed an interest in that.

It is very important. It is part of a larger strategy of being able to get commercial satellites affordable access to space, which is critical to our competitiveness in the larger telecommunications and remote sensing industries that are emerging.

Our ability to have assured access involves looking at foreign launches, but it also means balancing the interests, of minimizing the impact of the emerging market economies, such as Russia, the Ukraine and China, economies in transition, of minimizing the disruption of the market by allowing our industries to fairly compete, while on the other hand allowing the satellite and the applications users assured access to space by using them.

We think we hit that balance, and it is always a tough thing. But it is always a part of the larger strategy with regard to the President's space transportation policy.

And finally, the fourth issue is emerging markets. Particularly in the Commerce Department, we are very concerned, and I think it is part of our mandate as government.

One of the things we do well is collect information, and we have to be in a position of identifying emerging trends, where things are going in terms of the commercial launch industry, where should we frankly not impose regulations that could kill and industry before it emerges.

I think we see that in commercial use of GPS, global positioning satellites, for example. We don't want to do anything that kills that. It is now a fact that the commercial use of GPS exceeds the military use for which it was designed. There are just a lot of commercial users out there.

The same with spaceports, dual use technologies, state and Federal partnerships with regard to using those dual use facilities, the use of satellites in the GII and the NII, also very critical, and the emergence of these LEO constellations, which will allow for mobile global communications.

It is a very exciting era. It is a new era, and I think that we will be looking back now to see how we have made that transition between the 20th century and the 21st century.

And information technology, such as remote sensing and global communications, are critical to that. And the importance of protecting at a commercial level our interests in commercial space, as this emerges, I think is also something which is very critical.

So I thank you for the opportunity here today, Mr. Chairman, and I look forward to any questions you have.

Senator BURNS. Thank you.

[The prepared statement of Mr. Calhoun-Senghor follows:]

TESTIMONY OF
KEITH CALHOUN-SENGHOR
DIRECTOR, OFFICE OF AIR & SPACE COMMERCIALIZATION
U.S. DEPARTMENT OF COMMERCE

BEFORE THE

SUBCOMMITTEE ON SCIENCE, TECHNOLOGY AND SPACE
COMMITTEE ON COMMERCE, SCIENCE, AND TRANSPORTATION
UNITED STATES SENATE

MARCH 1, 1995

INTRODUCTION: Thank you, Mr. Chairman, and members of the Subcommittee, for the opportunity to testify before you today on the commercial space-related programs within the Department of Commerce's (DOC) Office of Air and Space Commercialization (OASC) as well as the President's FY 1996 Budget Request for those activities. I will also address the accomplishments and goals of the OASC as it relates to DOC's goal in affecting these policies.

BACKGROUND: As part of the Office of the Secretary, it is OASC's responsibility to advise the Secretary and Deputy Secretary on the formulation and implementation of policies related to commercial space. These policies are developed to foster the growth and international competitiveness of the U.S. commercial space sector, and promote the commercial use of space by U.S. private industry.

With the recent explosion of growth in commercial space, we deal with the following issues in anticipation of the future: traditional uses of space such as remote sensing and telecommunications; emerging markets and launch applications such as the commercial use of the Global Positioning System (GPS) and the potential for commercial production in space; and, space launch and transportation concerns such as international launch trade agreements and the policies regarding next generation space launch vehicle development.

To accomplish DOC's goals in these areas, OASC works with the private sector, other Federal agencies, state and other governmental entities to develop national policy with respect to the commercial use of space. OASC also coordinates policies on commercial space related activities within the various bureaus in the Commerce Department, including the Bureau of Export Administration (BXA), International Trade Administration (ITA), National Oceanic and Atmospheric Administration (NOAA), National Telecommunications and Information

Administration (NTIA), Technology Administration (TA), and Office of General Counsel (OGC).

**INVESTMENT IN THE FUTURE:** Over the last two years, OASC's accomplishments have included the President's policy on commercial satellite remote sensing and the President's National Space Transportation Policy. We have also been involved in a number of on-going initiatives like the U.S.-China Launch Trade Agreement, the Dual Use Launch Infrastructure Grant Program, the Aeronautics and Space Report of the President, as well as the Orbital Debris and Space Nuclear Power interagency working groups.

The total OASC Budget Request for FY 1996 is $457,000 and 4 personnel. With that budget, OASC will attend to the Department's priorities of executing the President's policy on commercial satellite remote sensing, implementing the space transportation policy, finalizing the space launch trade agreement with China, negotiating an agreement with Ukraine, and publishing *Space Business Indicators* , a compilation of commercial space market trends and information.

In this regard, it is important to point out Mr. Chairman, that at DOC and throughout the Federal Government, we are re-examining our mission through the National Performance Review. We are seeking customer input and asking whether our mission could be accomplished without Federal involvement, what the benefits of competition are, and how we can cut red tape and empower employees.

I would like to review for you some of the Department's major policy initiatives, giving you a sense of our accomplishments as well as what we have planned for the future.

**REMOTE SENSING:** In March, 1994, Deputy Secretary of Commerce David J. Barram, on behalf of the Administration, announced a major policy change in the treatment of commercial remote sensing imagery and systems. The U.S. Policy on Foreign Access to Remote Sensing Space Capabilities allows for expanded sales of commercial images from space and the potential for the export of remote sensing systems.

This policy represents a major milestone in the commercialization of space-based imagery and unleashes the potential of a critical 21st century information technology at a time when the international market for space-based imagery appears poised for significant expansion. It should open the way for U.S. aerospace firms to aggressively compete in what currently is a $400 million market worldwide, a market which could grow to more than $2 billion by the year 2000.

The geographic information systems (GIS) market, which provides end-use images incorporating demographic or technical data with digital maps, could be in the range of $5 to $15 billion by the turn of the century. Digital remote sensing images are a primary input to this market, and therefore drive the of the cost and quality of its product.

The data produced by remote sensing and GIS technology will include environmental and geographic information that will greatly advance emergency management and rescue, disaster relief, mineral exploration, crop management, cartography, marketing, real estate and a variety of other commercial endeavors and become an important product to be delivered over the National Information Infrastructure (NII) and Global Information Infrastructure (GII).

The remote sensing policy also aids the defense industry in its efforts to find new commercial applications for defense technologies.

In less than a year since the policy was released, NOAA's National Environmental Satellite Data Information Service (NESDIS), has granted five operator licenses to U.S. firms for the operation of commercial satellite remote sensing systems. A total of seven U.S. licenses have been issued since January of 1993.

The Department will continue to foster the U.S. technological lead in this area, encouraging U.S. preeminence in the worldwide commercialization of high resolution imagery, as the U.S. is not alone in the satellite data provision field. The European Space Agency, France, Russia, Japan, and India already have satellite remote sensing capabilities, and the press has recently reported that Israel, Korea, China, and Canada have plans to enter the commercial satellite remote sensing field. We will continue to work closely with the Departments of State and Defense, the intelligence community, and industry in the implementation and refinement of this policy, balancing economic, national security, and foreign policy concerns.

**SPACE LAUNCH TRADE AGREEMENTS:** OASC, in coordination with ITA, also represented the Department, working with the Office of the United States Trade Representative, Department of Transportation, State Department, and others in the U.S. government, as well as industry, to help increase the size of the world market for space launch without jeopardizing economic advantages that the United States has gained in satellite production.

Launch-service trade agreements developed with the governments of Russia and China strive for an environment under which introduction of launch vehicles from economies in transition will cause minimal economic disruption to the international launch market. These agreements will allow U.S. launch service providers to compete fairly with foreign providers for international business, will allow satellite constellation operators assured access to launch capability, and will aid the transition of formerly non-market economies to economies based on fair trade.

Just last month, the Department participated in the initialing of a new agreement with China. The formal signing will take place in the near future. Both that agreement, and the Russian launch agreement signed in 1993, call for annual consultations. OASC will be taking part in that process and will be working the Office of the U.S. Trade Representative on a possible new agreement with the government of Ukraine later this year.

In FY 1996 and the coming years, OASC will be involved in the monitoring and implementation of the agreements already signed, as well as in negotiations of possible new agreements with other non-market foreign launch providers. The Department views these agreements as an integral part of the Administration's plan to develop low-cost, dual use, reliable access to space and foster fair competition in the international launch market.

**NATIONAL SPACE TRANSPORTATION POLICY:** The recent Presidential policy on space transportation (U.S. National Space Transportation Policy, NSTC-4) explicitly recognizes the importance of private sector input into government space launch policies and activities. As a result, the President's policy mandates that the Department of Commerce and the Department of Transportation do two things:

1. explore new and innovate relationships between the government and the private sector, and

2. assure private sector involvement in the development of vehicles.

In response to the policy, OASC worked with Deputy Secretary Barram to organize a government-industry roundtable of 25 CEO's from the launch, satellite manufacturing and satellite operating community. The goal of the meeting was to listen to private-sector concerns and suggestions on ways in which industry and government could work together to get industry more involved in the design, development, and operation of our next generation launch vehicles.

As a result of this meeting, OASC and the Department of Transportation's Office of Commercial Space Transportation are refining a policy implementation plan that spells out specific means of promoting the international competitiveness of our space transportation sector. With industry, the National Aeronautics and Space Administration (NASA), the Department of Defense, and the Congress, the Departments of Commerce and Transportation will examine the role of the private sector in the design, financing and development of U.S. next generation launch systems, exploring innovative industry/government arrangements like risk sharing, tax incentives, equity participation, and antitrust exemption.

The Administration is also working to see that the commercial voice is heard in the initial stages of the government acquisition of launch vehicles. Through the National Spacelift Requirements Process, an interagency working group consisting of representatives from the Departments of Defense, Commerce, and

Transportation, NASA, and the intelligence community, we plan to develop a common set of spacelift system requirements that capture the needs of the defense, intelligence, civil, and commercial space sector. These common requirements, ranging in concept from "mass to orbit" to "customer satisfaction", will influence the future development of medium to heavy launch vehicles.

We feel that the future of the U.S. launch industry, and the ability of the U.S. government to get to space economically and reliably, depends on the kind of industry-government partnership we have begun under this policy.

**EMERGING MARKET TRENDS:** Technological innovation and scientific know-how are leading to new and exciting space-based activities at a breathtaking pace. We have seen this in the commercial application of Global Positioning System (GPS) information, the development of world-wide wireless communications constellations, and the advent of dual use launch facilities known as Space Ports.

OASC will keep an eye on future trends in commercial space not only by supporting the development of unique and innovative space applications where possible, but also by providing market information for making important space business choices. Our plans include investigating ways to remove impediments to a privately-financed, next generation commercial space-based production facility; consulting with private GPS equipment manufacturers to examine the application of GPS technology to the National and Global Information Infrastructure (GII), as well as investigating the every day utility of accurate, world-wide position information; and examining the role of satellites and wireless communication in the GII. We will also produce an updated edition of *Space Business Indicators*, a 1992 publication that highlights trends in the commercial space arena.

In closing, Mr. Chairman, Secretary Brown has made a commitment to promote the growth of U.S. high tech industry. We at the Office of Air & Space Commercialization are continuing that commitment by encouraging the cutting-edge advances made in commercial space while at the same time supporting U.S. national interests for ourselves, and for our children.

Senator BURNS. Mr. Weaver, it is nice to have you with us this morning.

## STATEMENT OF FRANK C. WEAVER, DIRECTOR, OFFICE OF COMMERCIAL SPACE TRANSPORTATION, U.S. DEPARTMENT OF TRANSPORTATION

Mr. WEAVER. Well, thank you very much, Mr. Chairman. It is good to be here and good to see you again.

I, too, would also like to submit my full written testimony for the record and make a few brief comments which summarize my testimony.

Senator BURNS. Without objection.

Mr. WEAVER. Thank you. Let me also begin by thanking you and the members of this subcommittee and your staff for this opportunity to discuss our program and our fiscal year 1996 budget.

On behalf of Secretary Peña, we at the Department of Transportation and the Office of Commercial Space Transportation look forward to continuing to work with all of you closely to help shape our nation's future in commercial space.

This is a challenging period in the commercial space industry. In 1984, when my office was established and as a result of the Commercial Space Launch Act, the United States was the dominant supplier of the world's launch market.

At the end of 1994, some 10 years later, we find that Europe's Arianespace is the dominant supplier in the international launch market.

So our goal is to work with other government agencies, with industry and with you to restore the U.S. launch industry as the leading supplier of commercial launch services in the international launch market.

Now the authority and the function of my office to meet this goal are twofold. First, per the Commercial Space Launch Act, we will regulate the U.S. space transportation industry so that we can protect the safety of the public and of property so as to prevent the unfortunate and tragic accident which recently happened during an explosion of a Chinese rocket, in which six people were killed and twenty-three people were injured.

DOT is the regulatory agency that is responsible for regulating other modes of transportation. Moving payloads to and from space is another mode of transportation.

And that is why we at the Department of Transportation, which is where I think we effectively belong, are working vigorously to fulfill one of the key missions of my office, and that is to ensure safety. We share the same opinions and views that you do about the safety of this industry.

Our second function is per the National Space Transportation Policy, which was signed by President Clinton in August 1994.

We, along with my colleague at the Department of Commerce, are to help enhance the international competitiveness of the launch industry.

We are developing an implementation plan, along with the Department of Defense and NASA, to make those vehicle systems that are being developed more commercially competitive, so that they also meets the needs of our national security and civil space sectors.

To fulfill these goals and objectives, my office is requesting a 1996 budget of $6,541,000. This is an increase of $534,000, or 9 percent, over our 1995 appropriation.

Three-fourths of this amount will be used for personnel compensation to fund for the full-year positions that were authorized in 1995's budget process. In 1996, we do not seek any additional personnel increases.

I would also like to take a few moments now to tell you about some of the key activities that we are undertaking in 1995. The first area is in launching and launch site regulations.

We are in the process of updating the regulations that were developed when our office was established and amended in 1988, to reflect the development of new space systems and the development of new commercial spaceports that were not completely addressed or adequately addressed at the time these regulations were developed.

The second area is in international trade in space launches. My office helps the U.S. trade representative negotiate agreements which promote market stability and competition as China, Russia and other international launch suppliers into the world space launch market.

In fact, my office heads the inter-agency working groups on information, which monitor the compliance of these foreign launch suppliers with the terms and conditions in these agreements.

A third area is in vehicle technology. The Department of Transportation chairs the Committee on Transportation Research and Development of the National Science and Technology Council.

Our deputy secretary, Mortimer Downey, chairs this committee. I chair the space launch working group, comprised of the Department of Defense, NASA, the Departments of Commerce and Energy, to coordinate launch vehicle research and development.

We also work closely with the Department of Defense, NASA and Commerce to develop a common set of space lift requirements that serve the civil, commercial and national security sectors.

Another area and activity is in space launch infrastructure. We must also have more cost efficient vehicles, as well as the adequate infrastructure to support the demand for launch services that we see increasing in the near term.

We are working closely with the U.S. private sector, existing DOD and NASA launch sites, and emerging commercial spaceports in California, Florida, New Mexico, Alaska and other interested state governments, to develop capabilities to support a variety of launch vehicle options.

Our vision for the future. We see commercial space as a growing industry with several new satellite services on the horizon. In 1994, the geostationary satellite communications was a $6.5 billion international industry, of which $580 million was space launch revenue of the U.S.

By the turn of the century, global mobile communication satellite systems, including those geostationary and low-earth-orbit systems, are projected to represent a $20 billion industry. $11 billion of the

$20 billion will represent satellites, launches and ground equipment.

The leadership position that the U.S. currently enjoys in providing these satellites and their services will require the United States to also have reliable and cost-effective launch capability, because if we are to establish the global information infrastructure and the national information infrastructure, we must be able to supply the complete package, and not be totally reliant upon foreign launch supply.

It is essential that the cost of access to space become a key ingredient in making sure we achieve this goal.

We also believe that the evolved expendable launch vehicle program and family should become operational around the turn of the century. And until that happens, we will need to upgrade the current ELVs in order to stay competitive.

We also think that the reusable launch vehicles, such as the single-stage-to-orbit (SSTO) is a promising technology to bring about a reduction in the cost to reach space.

Now, all of these new space systems, technologies and emerging spaceports pose an increasing burden on my office, because when these systems become commercial, it will be the responsibility of my office to certify them, to make sure that they operate safely, and to protect the public and property of the government.

Finally, Mr. Chairman, as part of the President's reinventing government initiative, we at all Federal agencies are reexamining our mission.

We are seeking customer input as we ask whether the mission could be accomplished without Federal investment and what the benefits of competition are.

This concludes my remarks. And once again, I thank you, the members and your staff for this opportunity. And I am available for any questions.

Senator BURNS. Thank you, Mr. Weaver.

[The prepared statement of Mr. Weaver follows:]

# STATEMENT

## OF

### FRANK C. WEAVER
### DIRECTOR
### OFFICE OF COMMERCIAL SPACE TRANSPORTATION
### U.S. DEPARTMENT OF TRANSPORTATION

## BEFORE THE

## UNITED STATES SENATE

## COMMITTEE ON
## COMMERCE, SCIENCE AND TRANSPORTATION

## SUBCOMMITTEE ON
## SCIENCE, TECHNOLOGY AND SPACE

## MARCH 1, 1995

## INTRODUCTION

Good morning Chairman Burns and members of the Subcommittee on Science, Technology and Space. I appreciate the opportunity to testify here today and to tell you of some of the exciting things that are going on in commercial space transportation and some of the areas we feel need to be addressed. And, since this hearing is preparatory to authorization of the Fiscal Year 1996 budget, I will address what we see as the resource needs to enable us to carry out our responsibilities in ensuring the U.S. safe, economical, and assured commercial access to space.

Mr. Chairman, I know that you and the members of this subcommittee are familiar with the history of commercial space operations in this country, but in view of the significant number of new members of the Senate as a whole this year, please permit me to recount a brief history of this industry for the record.

## BACKGROUND

From the beginning of the space age until relatively recently, space launching in this country was a strictly government activity, with NASA launching both scientific and commercial payloads and the military carrying out its own programs.

In the early 1980's, some visionaries dreamed of a commercial, private sector, space transportation industry and endeavored to make it a reality, leading to the recognition of the need for some coherent government oversight and regulatory focus, rather than the fragmented and debilitating need to deal

2

with various government concerns and requirements piecemeal.
Among the results were the Commercial Space Launch Act (CSLA) of
1984 and the establishment of the Office of Commercial Space
Transportation (OCST) within the Department of Transportation
(DOT).

Why DOT? some have asked. Two very logical reasons. Moving
non-government payloads, whether they are communications
satellites, scientific instruments, or ultimately people, to,
through, or from space is transportation. And this is a
potentially hazardous activity, as tragically demonstrated by the
recent failure of a Chinese space launch, killing six and
injuring 23 people in a village several miles away. DOT is the
regulatory agency which traditionally oversees the safety and
other concerns of transportation modes in this country.

Through this Act and subsequent policy decisions, OCST was
given the responsibility of ensuring the safety of commercial
space transportation through a process of licensing commercial
space launches and the operation of launch site facilities,
determining insurance requirements for launch operators,
facilitating access to government launch facilities, advising
other government agencies on the vehicle and infrastructure needs
of the commercial launch sector, and in various ways promoting
the growth and international competitiveness of the U.S.
commercial space transportation industry.

Little happened at first in this country, due to the
apparent availability of low cost shuttle launches and related

shutdown of expendable launch vehicle (ELV) production lines. However, the European Space Agency nations, having acted on their determination not to be dependent upon the shuttle, had developed their Ariane expendable launch vehicle and were already operating an alternative to the shuttle out of Kourou, French Guiana.

The Challenger disaster in 1986 led to the recognition that the launching of commercial payloads was not the best use of the shuttle and the decision by McDonnell Douglas, General Dynamics and other traditional U.S. launch vehicle manufacturers to go back into production and become commercial launch service providers. The CSLA gave them the ability to use federal, primarily military, launch sites on a direct cost reimbursement basis.

Restarting ELV production lines took time, however, and the first commercial licensed launch did not take place until early 1989, more than three years after the Challenger tragedy. In the meantime, with no Western alternative, the ESA Ariane rocket built up an early lead in launch contracts which set the stage for its current position of leadership in commercial launching.

The challenge before us today is to restore the U.S. to its long-held position as the dominant supplier of launch services to the world.

**CURRENT STATUS OF THE COMMERCIAL SPACE LAUNCH INDUSTRY**

From that 1989 start, the U.S. commercial space launch industry has grown. In spite of a few failures in a young and complex undertaking, the industry appears on the verge of

attaining a degree of maturity. We have had 45 licensed
commercial launches to date, including 15 each on Atlas and Delta
vehicles. Launch operations have taken place from Cape Canaveral
Air Station in Florida, White Sands Missile Range in New Mexico,
Vandenberg Air Force Base in California, Wallops Flight Facility
in Virginia, and the Kauai Test Facility in Hawaii.

Launch vehicles, such as the Atlas and Delta, have been
significantly improved in performance, payload capacity, and on-
orbit accuracy. New vehicles have been introduced or are under
development. Two licensed commercial launches have occurred
already this year and our commercial space launch manifest lists
17 more launches scheduled for the remainder of this calendar
year, although some of these could slip.

### A LOOK AHEAD.

In spite of this growth and progress in the last five years,
we believe the next twenty years will witness more significant
changes in space commerce than those which have occurred since
the dawn of the space age. We are excited about the long-range
outlook for the commercial space transportation segment. We have
a vision of space as a place to do business, and to do it in an
increasingly commercial manner. On the present course,
commercial space launches annually will potentially outnumber
government launches within the next few years, and we believe
this trend will continue.

Satellite communications is already a $6.5 billion (1994)
international industry, of which $580 million and growing

represents the U.S. commercial space launch industry. The industry has depended primarily on geostationary (GEO) satellites 22,300 miles above the equator, and these continue to be a mainstay. But now mobile systems to carry individual voice and data communications through constellations of numerous low-earth-orbiting (LEO) satellites are poised to add a whole new dimension to the industry. The FCC recently approved licenses for the Iridium, Globalstar, and Odyssey LEO systems to go with the previously approved Orbcomm system. A significant number of these satellites are expected to be launched aboard U.S. vehicles.

By the turn of the century, global mobile communications satellite systems and services, including geostationary and non-geostationary, are projected to represent a $20 billion market, of which $11 billion would be satellites, launches and ground equipment.

Companies are already well into plans to exploit the many benefits to be gained from earth imaging from space. These include environmental monitoring, agricultural assessment, mineral exploration, and even traffic management.

New and increasingly commercial uses of Global Positioning System (GPS) satellites are being developed, and satellites committed to data transmission and paging are ready for launching.

And, of course, there is the essential contribution that satellites will continue to make to the development of the

National and Global Information Infrastructures (NII and GII) through the unique capability they add in connecting anyone with anyone else, anywhere on the globe.

We in the U.S. will have control over our own access to these many benefits only as long as we have reliable and cost effective launch capability and capacity.

We look forward to the day when work will actually be done in space on a commercial basis and when travel to, through and from space will be routine. This is, of course, looking well into the future, but decisions we make now will do much to determine whether the United States and its business community will lead the way.

Manufacturing and technology development, materials processing and crystal growth in space are ideas which need to be pursued for commercial applications. Some may not prove economically feasible, or may be further in the future than we now see, but if this nation and our private sector do not lead the way, others will.

## NATIONAL SPACE TRANSPORTATION POLICY

On August 5, 1994, the Clinton Administration announced a new National Space Transportation Policy, and the White House, the Department of Transportation (DOT), and the Department of Commerce (DOC), are currently finishing up details on an implementation plan. This policy built on earlier work, (such as the Augustine Report and the Moorman Study), in which OCST participated, and also reflects input from our Commercial Space

Transportation Advisory Committee (COMSTAC), which provides
industry expertise and perspective to the Secretary of
Transportation.

I believe this policy and implementation plan provide the
context within which we, in partnership with Congress, can take
those steps needed to ensure the health and international
competitiveness of the U.S. space transportation industry.

The plan lays out the roles and responsibilities of
government departments and agencies, and other witnesses will,
I'm sure, address some of these. We, at Transportation, have the
primary responsibility for addressing the international
competitiveness of the U.S. launch industry, and, with the
Department of Commerce, developing public/private partnerships
that will cooperate with NASA and the Department of Defense in
their respective development of the next generation reusable
launch vehicles and the evolved expendable launch vehicle (EELV)
family.

Until the EELV family becomes operational, upgrades to the
traditional expendable launch vehicle fleet are essential in
order to stay competitive, an important interim step while
awaiting the next generation vehicles. These measures are needed
in order for launch providers to remain competitive in the short
run, and to reduce the government's own launch costs during that
period.

OCST also participated in the grant selection process for
the 1993 and 1994 Air Force Dual-Use Infrastructure Grant

Programs.

## RE-USABLE LAUNCH VEHICLES

We believe that the re-usable launch vehicle, such as the single-stage-to-orbit (SSTO) concept, is a promising technology to bring about a reduction in the cost to reach space. Such vehicles have the potential to provide highly reliable, safe and economical access to space.

There are, in fact, some promising entrepreneurial efforts underway along these lines. We are following closely the efforts of small, risk-taking private firms, which are actually building hardware with private capital to demonstrate their vision of how this can be done.

DOT is conducting pre-license consultations with larger, well-established commercial companies that are developing reusable launch vehicle technology in an effort to acquaint them with licensing requirements. We are advising them on approaches to safety issues and other considerations that may involve vehicle design, operation, and maintenance. In doing so we are establishing government/industry partnerships that will define the approaches to be used in shifting from high cost, infrequent, access to space, to lower cost, frequent, access, while protecting public health and safety.

## TECHNOLOGICAL INNOVATION

Companies such as American Rocket, with its pioneering work on hybrid propellant, Orbital Sciences Corporation, developer of

the air-launched Pegasus and other innovations, and the
Commercial Experiment Transporter (COMET) orbital re-entry
vehicle, are only a few examples of the private sector pushing
the technological envelope.

In another approach, we are working with a major U.S.
aerospace firm pursuing an innovative commercial launch concept
that involves collaboration among partners in this country,
Russia, Ukraine, and Norway. This new "sea launch" venture would
operate out of a U.S. home port and use a mobile floating launch
platform to provide the optimum launch location for each specific
kind of satellite.

### REGULATORY ISSUES

These new technologies pose new and unique safety/regulatory
issues. No longer is the government necessarily performing
technical oversight over design and development of these new
vehicles and technologies. DOT is the government agency
responsible for assuring public health and safety as concerns the
operation of these vehicles in commercial transportation and we
must develop new expertise and regulatory tools to keep pace
with the evolving changes occurring in this industry.

The development of industry standards is a desirable goal to
increase efficiency and streamline both industry operations and
the regulatory process. To stimulate and focus industry interest
in such standards, OCST sponsored a workshop under the auspices
of the American Institute of Aeronautics and Astronautics to
address the benefits to the international space transportation

industry.  I am pleased to report that this effort is on-going, with plans to have the first range safety standards available for industry review later this spring.  We believe this will become a springboard to streamlining the regulation of the commercial space transportation industry by allowing the industry to define the standards by which it will provide for safe and reliable space systems.

During 1995, DOT is considering a number of activities to help achieve this vision of commercial space transportation in the next two decades.   Allow me to mention a few:

o  Launching and Launch Site Regulations:  DOT hopes to update regulations concerning commercial launches and the operation of commercial  launch sites.  Using information gathered at a public meeting in October 1994, we intend to enhance both the definition and clarity of the 1988 regulations while retaining the flexibility necessary to encompass new space transportation systems developed since then.

o  International Trade in Space Launches: DOT has helped to negotiate international agreements which promote market stability and competition as China and Russia enter the world space launch market and transition to market economies.  OCST leads the interagency Working Groups on Information, which are responsible for monitoring Chinese and Russian compliance with the agreements.  We are analyzing the need for international agreements with market economies (e.g., Europe and Japan) to provide for free and fair competition in space launches.  OCST

11

supports the USTR by conducting LEO and GEO market assessments enabling the USTR to allow foreign launch suppliers to participate without disrupting the market.

o Vehicle Technology: DOT is working closely with DOD, NASA, and DOC to develop a common set of spacelift requirements to serve civil, commercial, and national security needs. DOT is also working closely with the other agencies to develop a coordinated technology plan to serve the future needs of the three space sectors.

o Space Launch Infrastructure: DOT is working closely with the U.S. private sector, existing DOD and NASA launch sites, emerging commercial spaceports, and interested state governments to develop an inventory of the infrastructure needs of the commercial space transportation industry.

We, at DOT, view our role as ensuring the safety of commercial space transportation. As you may recall, I requested the DOT Inspector General to review the procedures, processes, and organizational structure of the Licensing and Safety Division of OCST. Copies of the IG's report and our implementation plans for the recommendations made were provided to members of the subcommittee last year. We are well on our way to implementing those recommendations. We are in the process of updating the regulations, providing for electronic communications with our constituents, automation of the license application process, expanding our in-house expertise (three added personnel in 1994 brought in excess of 70 years aerospace experience to the

office), and enhancement of two-way communications between the
licensing staff and license applicants.

Our goal is to work with industry. We welcome innovation and
enterprise, commensurate with our responsibility to maintain
safety. We also want to provide clarification to the site
operator licensing process to facilitate development of this new
industry and associated services.

### INFRASTRUCTURE

Transportation infrastructure is, after safety, the
principal operational concern of DOT, and space transportation
infrastructure is probably undergoing, proportionately, the
greatest transformation of any mode of transportation. While
commercial launches to date have all taken place from federal
facilities, work is proceeding on planning and development of
four commercial launch sites in the U.S.

- Western Commercial Space Center located at Vandenberg
Air Force Base in California has just received a $30
million investment from ITT and plans to support a
variety of small launch vehicle operations.
- Spaceport Florida Authority is developing one or more
commercial launch sites at Cape Canaveral and
elsewhere.
- Alaska Spaceport plans development at Kodiak Island
that would support commercial polar-orbital and
suborbital launches.
- Southwest Regional Spaceport adjacent to White Sands

13

Missile Range in New Mexico is planning to support
commercial sounding rocket activity and new reusable
and expendable launch vehicle systems. It was the site
for testing McDonnell Douglas's Delta Clipper, a single-
stage-to-orbit concept vehicle.

DOT has the statutory responsibility to ensure protecting
public health and safety through licensing operation of these
facilities and is looking at innovative partnerships and other
ways to be supportive of these groundbreaking undertakings.

We look to the implementation of other strategies, such as
anchor tenancy, termination liability, innovative partnerships,
and imaginative tax policies for commercial launch providers and
spaceport developers to leverage private capital into space
commerce.

### FY '96 BUDGET REQUEST

Against this backdrop, Mr. Chairman, I note the President's
FY 1996 request for the Office of Commercial Space Transportation
is $6.541 million. It represents an increase of $534 thousand,
or 9%, over the final FY 1995 appropriation. Three quarters of
this amount is for personnel compensation, to fund for the full
year positions authorized in the FY 1995 budget process. The FY
1996 request does not seek any additional personnel.

The FY 1995 staffing increases were enacted in response
to the demands placed on OCST by the growth in the commercial
space launch industry and its increasing complexity and

14

diversity. It is responding to industry's desire for more
explicit guidance concerning licensing requirements.

Future resource needs are difficult to predict in a climate
of diversifying technology and proprietary developments that can
suddenly make yesterday's projection obsolete. A radical
development in new vehicle technology, a dramatic breakthrough on
cost per pound to orbit or other development could greatly alter
the Office's requirements to be able to ensure safe and
environmentally responsible commercial space transportation.

As part of the President's Reinventing Government
Initiative, we, and all federal agencies, are reexamining our
mission. We are seeking "customer" input, as we ask whether the
mission could be accomplished without federal investment, what
the benefits of competition are, and ways to cut red tape and
empower employees.

This concludes my formal remarks. Once again, I thank you
for inviting me to testify this morning. I would be happy to
answer any of your questions.

###

Senator BURNS. We will just start with you. There are a couple of questions that I will ask both of you. I would also—there will be some questions from other committee members that you might respond to the committee and to the individual committee members at a later date. We will keep the record open, as far as this hearing is concerned.

Secretary Peña is planning for a total reorganization of DOT as a part of the effort to reinvent government. And it is my understanding that under that plan, Mr. Weaver, your office would be abolished and its functions will be transferred to the FAA.

Would you comment on the Secretary's plan at this point, as it relates to your office?

Mr. WEAVER. OK, Mr. Chairman. Let me just clarify one point.

Senator BURNS. OK.

Mr. WEAVER. And that is that Secretary Peña has announced the consolidation of the existing ten modes at the Department of Transportation into three broad categories. Those categories would be air, land and maritime.

What he has proposed is relocating my office from the Office of the Secretary into one of those groupings that he refers to as air. He does not intend to abolish my office, but simply to locate it in a grouping along with the FAA.

Mr. David Hinson, the Administrator of the FAA, and I just met last week. I can assure you that Mr. Hinson is an avid supporter of space, and he intends to work closely with me to continue to make sure that my office can perform the functions.

So at the present time, it is not being abolished. We are working to develop a proposal, which we will be submitting to Congress for legislative changes. And at that time, I will be happy to meet with you and other members of the committee when we can discuss this in more detail.

Senator BURNS. Do you have a timeframe on that, when that will happen, or any indication of that?

Mr. WEAVER. The indication is that by mid–March, we will have a series of legislative proposals that will be submitted to the respective transportation oversight committees. And at that time, we will be able to discuss the entire DOT restructuring program with Members of Congress.

Senator BURNS. I would say in this government, it always seems like to me—and, of course, I am running into more over here.

I am more accustomed to doing business with Federal land managers and the challenges that we face over in Energy and Natural Resources, because we come from a resource state. And we find a lot of departments that do not talk to one another.

There is no communication. The right hand does not know what the left hand is doing. So we all start out in this business of cutting our own trail, so to speak.

In the ongoing—and I congratulate you interacting with Mr. Calhoun-Senghor over in the Commerce Department, because I think it is—one of these days we are going to have to lay down some lines of who is in charge here, so that we are not only talking to one another, we also—there is a clear line of authority whenever we start talking about the commercialization of space and the launching and this type of thing and how it affects this country.

There has been an ongoing debate between NASA and your office over which agency has jurisdiction over commercial launches of NASA payloads. NASA argues that when it purchases a commercial launch service, NASA has the legal right to waive OCST's jurisdiction over the launch.

In fact, NASA claims OCST has no jurisdiction whatsoever over these launches because they are not commercial. Are you working toward any kind of a resolution to this? And if you have, can you tell us what progress you have made?

Mr. WEAVER. Yes, I can, Mr. Chairman. My office has been working with NASA on the use of commercial launch services.

As a matter of fact, there is one program that NASA recently announced that will require bidders to obtain a commercial launch license. That was in the memorandum of agreement for the ultralight program.

There is another program that NASA had helped to sponsor, but it is a commercial program, the Comet program. And in that one, we issued a license to the launch company.

And then part of our request to update regulations is to seek more explicit authority to protect the public safety. Currently it is implied that we may have the authority for reentry, it is not explicitly required.

So yes, we are continuing to work with NASA to define the areas of cooperation. But when NASA seeks to launch its programs, and they have to procure expendable vehicles, that is where we do not have oversight.

But in those cases where they are truly commercial, we do cooperate with them, and we do license those lauches. And we do have a much more cooperative relationship.

If I may add, NASA is more enthusiastic about working with my office. And they mentioned that on the ultra-light program, before they issued an RFP, they wanted to require us to work with industry and for the industry to seek a license. So that cooperative spirit is working well.

Senator BURNS. Could you give us an insight on the agreement that is just about to be signed with China, limiting their—what they can charge and also their number of China launchings? Could you give us an insight on that agreement? I guess it has not been signed yet, I understand.

Mr. WEAVER. That is correct. It was initialed on January 27, 1995 subject to the mutual review of both governments, just for language translation. But it is subject to be signed in the very near future.

Senator BURNS. Give us some details. What will the U.S. launch industry—how do we gain from that agreement?

Mr. WEAVER. OK. Let me first state that this—negotiating this agreement involved very close cooperation and consultation with all sectors of the commercial space industry.

Both Mr. Calhoun-Senghor and I met with all sectors, the satellite manufacturers, launch vehicle manufacturers, and service providers, in developing the terms and conditions.

Briefly stated, what we have arrived at in this, I think, most comprehensive trade agreement is that in terms of the access that China will have to the geostationary market, we arrived at a quantity where they could have 11, up to 11, payloads to be launched over the 7-year term of the agreement.

And this is approximately equal to the same number that they had in the other agreement, if you look at launches per year.

In the low-earth-orbit market, we arrived at a discipline where, in the deployment of these global constellations, where there would be multiple launches and several dozen or more satellites to be launched, we arrived at terms and conditions which would look at the total participation by countries from economies that have economies in transition, to look at the relative share that they will have in the deployment of these systems.

And only if it exceeds the share that western market suppliers will have would we have a concern, and then we have stipulated key factors that would be considered: whether or not there was available launch supply from the West, whether or not they were key business decisions.

But we worked those terms so that industry would not be overly burdened, and they would at least have some guiding parameters to let them make the most effective business decision.

Also, to go back to the GEO quantity, we also developed a provision that would grandfather four more payloads, because the Chinese signed contracts before the old agreement expired, and they had not launched the entire quota that they were allowed under the terms of the first agreement.

We also developed what we call adjustment factors, because the industry had noted to us that there are certain costs which we were able to not only categorize but quantify, that are unique to launching in China, as opposed to launching in the United States or from Kourou on an Ariane rocket.

So we identified those factors, negotiated those with the Chinese government, and specified what they were and what the price ranges were.

We also arrived at a more, we thought, agreeable and also a more factual differential in order to look at the prices that Chinese launch suppliers would offer in the market.

That differential is at 15 percent, so that we would, considering those factors, not regard it necessary to look at each one as long as their price was within 15 percent of the lowest western bid.

But we would look at those factors in greater detail if there was a price that was offered outside that range and determine if those quantifiable price differences actually were more than what we thought they were.

We think that on balance this agreement will provide greater market stability. It will also allow U.S. satellite manufacturers to have access to launch vehicles from China and supply satellites in that region of the world where there is an increased demand for satellite service.

And it does not severely impact the launch vehicle manufacturers. So we tried to strike a balance between at times conflicting demands and the conflicting needs of those sectors of the industry.

Senator BURNS. Mr. Calhoun-Senghor, I understand the commercial sensoring market is about $700 million right now, and that is expected to really blow. Can you give us any idea on how big that market could be and its rate of development now?

Mr. CALHOUN-SENGHOR. Yes, sir, Mr. Chairman. The commercial mode sensing market is a very exciting market, because currently, as you know, most of what is being aimed at for U.S. companies entering this is the aerial photography market, a well-established market.

You are right. It is about $500 to $700 million currently. It is expected that, by the turn of the century, to be about $2 billion a year.

That does not include the geographic information systems, GIS, which is the integration of the information, demographic information, population information, on imagery.

If you include that, the software industry that that includes, and the processing, you are talking anywhere from $10 to $15, some have it as high as $20 billion per year.

It is a huge market. It is emerging. It is an established market. And judging from the number of companies that have applied for licenses with the Department, a lot of companies believe it is substantial.

Senator BURNS. It may sound silly, but with the development in this area of the capabilities of these systems, in other words, where they are constantly being upgraded all the time—just something pops in my head—is there any national security implications here, as we go down this road?

Mr. CALHOUN-SENGHOR. I think there are clearly, sir. And I think, also, they were clearly dealt with, anticipated and, I can assure you, heavily debated and resolved in the policy debate.

There is no question that there is a connection between the uses of this from a commercial point of view, as well as from a national security point of view.

It is information. That is part of what makes the information age that we are going into so exciting, but also so potentially challenging. What the policy did is it realized two things. It had a two-part strategy, to address your question.

The first is, it said, in order to meet the national security concerns, we had to ask ourselves an essential question: In time of crisis, where you have American troops on the ground or we have our allies at risk, who would you rather have overhead taking imagery, U.S.-controlled satellites where we have some leverage and, frankly, patriotism on the part of our companies, or would we rather have countries involved who may not share our same interests?

So it was important for us to unshackle U.S. industry to allow them to enter the market and thereby be a significant player.

That reduces, and hopefully significantly reduces, the economic incentive for other countries to endogenously develop that capability. That is the first part.

The second part of it is that there were some very, very well-thought-through national security conditions applied to these licenses.

This was a process which did not happen over a matter of months. In fact, it goes back, probably for the origins of discussion about commercial remote sensing, two administrations.

But what we did in the President's policy is we had the intelligence community, the Defense Department, Commerce Department and State Department all realizing that we are entering a new day and that what we had to do is, instead of pretending that there was no wide foreign availability to this, get ahead of the problem.

There are almost a dozen countries, Mr. Chairman, who have indigenous, technological capability to produce remote sensing capabilities and are getting actively involved in it commercially.

Therefore, what we did is, in our licenses, we required several things. First of all, we required that the U.S. Government, at a cabinet level decision, the Secretary of Commerce, the Secretary of State, the Secretary of Defense could, in time of crisis, essentially shut the system off, so that if we thought that U.S. national security were involved, we had—the President always had that option.

More realistically what we would want to do, however, is to deny access to the commercial customer and probably encrypt it in that situation to our forces. So we have done that.

The second thing—there are a number of things, but the other thing is that we have on all of these satellites an approved encryption device, approved by the government.

The changes in orbits, no change in the operational qualities of the satellite can occur without the approval of the government. Any significant agreement with a foreign customer has to be reviewed by the government.

We have essentially the whole panoply of options open to us. It was a fine balance between imposing such harsh restrictions that we essentially would drive away the customer base and therefore effectively keep us out of the market versus allowing for the U.S. national security to be protected.

But at the end of the day, the question that I believe made the intelligence community and defense community not only supporters, but enthusiastic supporters, are that they now have enhanced capability.

The strong presence of U.S. commercial companies reduces the economic incentive, gives us greater access to this imagery at cheaper prices, is a return on the investment of the American taxpayer, and increases information in an age where we have to be ahead of the problem as opposed to reacting to it.

So we have both of those, economic as well as national security concerns, and we had the ability, when our national security and those of our close friends and allies dictated, to deal with that in any way that we deem appropriate.

Senator BURNS. I would imagine there will be another committee or two up here on the Hill that will be interested in visiting with you on that particular matter.

Let's talk about the LEO COMSATS, the low orbits communications.

Mr. CALHOUN-SENGHOR. Yes, sir.

Senator BURNS. We are hearing now a lot of joint ventures now into that market. Both the Teledesic and the Iridium ventures have had to overcome some technical and financial hurdles.

But any technical problems are overshadowed by the problems the LEO COMSAT companies have had with government red tape and regulation. I am wondering are we—what regulatory actions must occur to allow these LEO COMSAT constellations to be built?

Rules and regulations are being developed now, or are they finalized? You might bring us up to date on what is being done there.

Mr. CALHOUN-SENGHOR. Well, Mr. Chairman, the largest—well, the initial hurdle that had to be cleared—some have already cleared it—is the spectrum allocation issue.

That is a very large issue. It is a precedent-setting issue, because once the spectrum is allocated to the United States, you have to have an international spectrum allocation.

The stakes involved in this are extremely high. Other countries realize that and currently have, I think, the initiative in this country, in terms of doing that, and so we want to make sure that we are, in our spectrum allocation decisions, that we allow the market to develop and for us to have that commercial and technological initiative rewarded.

That is something which is largely in the hands of the FCC. They have approved five of the initial big LEO companies for that.

After that, you get into some of the questions that Mr. Weaver just talked about: Access, affordable access to space. That is why the space transportation policy is so important.

That is why the launch agreements are so important, because you cannot make it a common-place business to have a telephone or a device that allows you to communicate if you cannot get your piece of equipment up there.

It is very important, I think, in terms of those kinds of regulations. We have to be very careful that we are, one, incentivizing private industry to develop, invest its own money to develop, launch vehicles. That is part of the President's strategy, to get the commercial companies involved.

We also have to be careful that we are not providing unintentionally disincentives for the commercial companies to get involved.

And that could be in terms of how we procure a vehicle or by setting the kinds of regulations or the kinds of procurement requirements which have no commercial application later.

That is frankly the job, the mandate, that the Presidential policy gave us. I think it is a very exciting time, in terms of global communications, for rural applications, for the transmission of imagery.

I think we have not begun to realize the possibilities if we combine imagery with global access to the Internet and with GPS and location data. It will tell you where the nearest school is, where the nearest pizza parlor is, tell you where your children are, put maps in your cars. It is very exciting, sir.

Senator BURNS. Well, we thank both of you for coming down today and offering your testimony. And again, we will leave the record open. And any of the members of this committee who want to ask questions and would want to submit them, you may respond to them and the committee. Thank you for coming today.

That concludes this hearing this morning. Thank you very much.

Mr. CALHOUN-SENGHOR. Thank you, Mr. Chairman.

Mr. WEAVER. Thank you, Mr. Chairman. (Whereupon, at 11:37 a.m., the hearing was adjourned.)

# APPENDIX

QUESTIONS ASKED BY SENATOR LARRY PRESSLER AND ANSWERS THERETO BY
MR. CALHOUN-SENGHOR

*Question 1.* Would you describe the size and character of today's remote sensing market both in the U.S. and globally? Who are the main international competitors in this market? Who purchases the remote sensing data, and for what reasons? What is your estimate of the growth potential for the commercial remote sensing market?

Answer. Industry has estimated the market for satellite remote sensing data, ground equipment, and value added services at nearly $500 million currently, and expects a market size of $2 billion by the close of the century. Prospective entrants to the market hope to capitalize on an even larger geographic information systems market with growth potential from $5 billion to $15 billion by the turn of the century. Increased technical capabilities, in terms of resolution, response time, and processing capability, are key to this projected economic expansion.

The data produced by this technology will include environmental and geographic information that will greatly advance emergency management and rescue, disaster relief, mineral exploration, crop management, cartography, marketing, real estate and a variety of other commercial endeavors and become an important product to be delivered over this country's National Information Infrastructure (NII) and Global Information Infrastructure (GII).

The United States is not alone in the satellite data provision field, however. The European Space Agency, France, Russia, Japan, and India already have commercial satellite remote sensing capabilities, and Korea, China, Canada, and Israel have plans to enter the satellite remote sensing field, and offer data on the commercial market.

*Question 2.* In 1992, I cosponsored the Land Remote Sensing Policy Act to allow U.S. companies to offer private remote sensing systems. How many U.S. companies have sought, or are seeking, licenses under the 1992 act? What is your office doing to increase the competitiveness of U.S. firms?

Answer. In March, 1994, under the authority of the Land Remote Sensing Policy Act, Deputy Secretary of Commerce David J. Barram, on behalf of the Administration, announced a major policy change in the treatment of commercial remote sensing imagery and systems. The U.S. Policy on Foreign Access to Remote Sensing Space Capabilities allows for expanded sales of commercial images from space.

Building on the intent of the Land Remote Sensing Policy Act, the new satellite remote sensing policy represents a major milestone in the commercialization of space-based imagery. It unleashes the potential of a critical 21st century information technology at a time when the international market for space-based imagery appears poised for significant expansion.

It also aids the defense industry in its efforts to find new commercial applications for defense technologies.

In less than a year since the policy was released, the Department of Commerce's National Oceanic and Atmospheric Administration (NOAA) has granted five operator licenses to U.S. firms for the operation of commercial satellite remote sensing systems. A total of seven U.S. licenses have been issued since January of 1993. These licenses were granted to: EOSAT (for the operation of Landsat 6, that failed to achieve orbit); Orbital Sciences Corporation for both the SeaStar and Eyeglass systems; Lockheed Missiles and Space; WorldView Imaging; Ball Aerospace; and AstroVision. There are currently two more license applications under consideration.

At OASC, we will continue to foster the U.S. technological lead in this area, encouraging U.S. preeminence in the worldwide commercialization of high resolution imagery. The Department of Commerce will work closely with industry, the Departments of Defense and State, and the Intelligence Community, in implementing this policy, balancing economic, national security, and foreign policy concerns.

*Question 3.* For twenty years, Landsat has provided the Nation with an uninterrupted flow of Earth images used in agriculture, research, mineral exploration, and land-use planning. What is your assessment of the current Landsat program? What role do you see Landsat playing in the increasingly competitive remote sensing market? What is the status of the development of the replacement Landsat (Landsat 7)?

Answer. Landsat is an important provider of satellite imagery from space for use in numerous scientific applications, as well as commercial applications that demand large scale overhead data. In the increasingly commercial world of satellite remote sensing, Landsat will continue to play a key role in providing continuous data for tracking climate change and global environmental trends, and the broad area coverage its sensors provide will offer diversity of resolution for use in commercial applications.

Landsat 7 is presently being developed by the Landsat Program Management consisting of the National Aeronautics and Space Administration (NASA), NOAA, and the United States Geological Survey (USGS). The Critical Design Review for the Landsat 7 spacecraft is expected to occur this fall and launch of the satellite is expected in the second half of calendar year 1998.

*Question 4.* Commercial remote sensing systems are offering data with increasingly higher resolution. What is the highest resolution offered commercially and who is providing it? Does the commercial availability of high-resolution satellites raise any security concerns for the U.S. and its allies, and, if so, what are they? How can these concerns be addressed?

Answer. The French Spot system of commercial remote sensing satellites currently offers 10 meter resolution satellite images compared with 30 meter data provided by Landsat. Recently, the Russians have begun offering 2 meter resolution data for sale commercially. These images are easily accessible from commercial vendors and over the Internet. Indications are that, independent of planned U.S. commercial entry into this field, the broadest commercial applications for such images require resolution of approximately one meter. Therefore, it is the stated goal of several foreign providers of imagery to compete in the one meter market.

In times of crisis, imagery of almost any resolution raises security concerns. The President's remote sensing policy addresses these concerns by providing for mechanisms to limit the collection and/or distribution of imagery from U.S. systems in times of crisis. However, remote sensing capabilities are no longer limited to two or three countries. Thus, the policy is intended support U.S. industry in their attempt to play a significant role in this market, so that in times of crisis it is U.S. satellites that are passing overhead.

In an era where satellite remote sensing images are an international commodity, protecting our national security means having U.S. firms be significant players in the international market for commercial imagery.

At present, U.S. companies have received licenses to operate remote sensing satellites with 1 meter resolution. Their operator licenses include a condition by which in times of crisis, the U.S. government has the authority to limit or shut-down these commercial systems, or, more importantly, encrypt their signals and down-link the imagery to commanders in the field of battle.

*Question 5.* The commercial space activities of your office overlaps considerably with those of DoT and NASA. Has any though been given to consolidating these activities under one agency?

Answer. The Office of Air & Space Commercialization is a highly efficient four person office whose mission is to assist the Secretary of Commerce in fostering the growth and international competitiveness of the commercial space industry.

The mission of the Department of Commerce with regard to space differs significantly from the missions of the Department of Transportation and NASA. Their primary missions are regulatory (launch safety regulation) and civil (administration of the civil space programs) respectively, while the Department of Commerce's principal mission is commercial—to work with industry to ensure and enhance economic opportunity for American firms.

The presence of a cabinet level voice for business, in this case commercial space, is of significant importance in the emerging commercial space industry where the role of government is decreasing and where policy decisions often affect whether emerging industries will have to compete with government programs. Such a policy role is key to job growth and economic expansion.

*Question 6.* What is your assessment of the recent U.S.-China launch agreement which regulates the number and pricing of China's commercial launches? Why is the agreement more favorable than the recent U.S.-Russia launch deal? What is the role of your office in the negotiation of these international launch agreements?

Answer. The follow-on U.S.-China Commercial Space Launch Trade Agreement reflects an appropriate balance between U.S. launch and satellite interests. With the ongoing consolidation of domestic launch capabilities in the medium to heavy class as well as the increase in international cooperation (from hardware, operational and marketing standpoints) it was critical to have sufficient flexibility written into the China agreement.

The terms of the China Agreement were the result of five rounds of intensive negotiations over several months, and reflect an extremely high degree of consultation with the U.S. launch and satellite industries. We believe the proper balance was struck and that the agreement reflects the commercial realities of the market.

The Office of Air & Space Commercialization has the primary responsibility of co-ordinating Department positions for the negotiating process and ongoing implementation. We are also the lead representative for the Department at the negotiating table.

---

*Question I.a.* What are the main activities of your office?

Answer. The Department of Transportation's Office of Commercial Space Transportation (OCST) is the Government agency responsible for ensuring the safety of the U.S. commercial space transportation industry and for supporting White House development of policy on national space transportation and international space launch trade. OCST licenses the private sector launching of payloads on expendable launch vehicles (ELVs) and commercial space launch facilities and sets liability insurance requirements for activities associated therewith. OCST is also charged with promoting and facilitating commercial space launches. It also provides a focal point in the Federal Government for formulating and implementing consistent policies that enable the commercial U.S. space transportation industry to compete in domestic and international markets.

Additionally, other major OCST activities include:
- updating regulations involving launch operations and launch sites;
- monitoring non-market economies' (NMES) compliance with international space launch trade agreements;
- supporting launch vehicle research and development study efforts; and
- identifying adequate space launch infrastructure to support increasing demands for launch services.

*Question I.b.* What is the status of Secretary Peña's announced plan to consolidate your office into the FAA?

Answer. Planning for OCST's transition to the FAA is well underway. More detail is anticipated later this Spring. Initial discussions intended to explore the appropriate structure within the proposed Aviation Administration for OCST have been initiated.

*Question I.c.* What is the time frame for that consolidation proposal?

Answer. Consolidation of OCST and the FAA is anticipated for early fiscal year 1996.

*Question I.d.* If your activities are moved to FAA, would those activities be changed in any way?

Answer. It is not expected that the mission for OCST as set forth in the 49 U.S.C. Subsection IX and the President's National Space Transportation Policy will change due to a restructured DOT.

*Question I.e.* Is there any discussion of moving your activities relating to promoting the U.S. commercial space industry to DoC?

Answer. There are no plans to move to the Department of Commerce any current OCST activities intended to regulate, promote, or facilitate the commercial space transportation industry.

*Question II.a.* How large is the world commercial launch market?

Answer. Commercial space is a growing industry with several new satellite services anticipated. In 1994, the geostationary satellite communications segment was a $6.5 billion international industry, of which $580 million was space launch revenue in the U.S. In addition to this segment by the turn of the century, global mobile communication satellite systems, including those geostationary (GEO) and low-earth-orbit (LEO) systems are projected to represent $20 billion. Eleven billion dollars of the $20 billion will represent satellites, launches and ground equipment.

The international market for commercial launch services to GEO for medium and large communications satellites currently consists of approximately 12 to 15 launches per year. The projected number of payloads available to all international launch competitors in the market is slightly higher at 14 to 16 per year, with the difference resulting from the effect of two satellites launched by a single rocket as practiced by Arianespace. This level of demand is expected to remain fairly constant through the year 2005.

The launch of small, low earth orbit (LEO) satellites will be the most dynamic segment of the international launch market. The total projected number of small international payloads (including "Big" and "Little" communications satellite systems, scientific, remote sensing, and microgravity) is expected to range between 200 and 250 payloads by the end of the decade. (source: OCST, "LEO Commercial Payload Projections, March 31, 1994.)

*Question II.b.* Who are the main competitors and what are their market shares?

Answer. In terms of international supply for GEO launches, commercial launch services for medium and large satellites are currently provided by Arianespace of Europe, McDonnell Douglas and Lockheed-Martin of the United States, China Great Wall Industry Corporation (CGWIC) of the People's Republic of China (PRC), and Lockheed-Khrunichev-Energia Incorporated (LKE) of Russia. Arianespace continues to lead with over 50 percent of the market of the internationally competed launches, followed by McDonnell Douglas and Lockheed-Martin with a combined share of approximately 35 percent. CGWIC has recently become more active, providing approximately 10 percent of the world's commercial launches, while LKE appears to have about 5 percent of the market. The U.S. industry also benefits from the commercial launching of payloads which are not internationally competed, as does Arianespace.

*Question II.c.* What other countries are expected to enter the market in the near future and what is the status of their efforts?

Answer. Ukraine is considering plans to enter the commercial space launch market by offering an upgraded Zenit space vehicle. Two joint projects involving US corporations are under way. Boeing plans to join with a Ukrainian rocket builder, Russian engine producer and Norwegian oil platform manufacturer in a US-based partnership. The Norwegian oil platform will be used for equatorial launches of the Zenit rocket and will be home ported in Long Beach, California.

The second project involves Rockwell and a Ukrainian rocket builder to launch Zenits initially to low earth orbit from Plesetsk, Russia.

*Question III.a.* How would you assess the competitiveness of the U.S. commercial launch industry?

Answer. Factors that characterize competition within the international medium/heavy launch market arena include: (1) the price of the launch service; (2) launch vehicle reliability and system operability; (3) schedule availability and dependability; and (4) weight lift capability. U.S. systems, in particular Atlas, are generally m9re price competitive with Ariane IV than with rockets from economies-in-transition [EIT]. Furthermore, over the past eight years, the Delta is considered the world's most reliable launch vehicles at 100 percent, although the Atlas-Centaur is also a leader in the area at 93%. These success rates compare favorably to those of foreign launch vehicles (the Russian Proton nearly 90%, the Chinese Long March 2E at 60%, and the European Ariane IV at about 90%).

Since Orbital Sciences Corporation's Pegasus launch of a Brazilian payload in early 1993, which became the first commercial, orbital launch of a small vehicle, the U.S. has the lead in this market niche. In anticipation of greater demand for launch services, many new small vehicle providers have emerged, such as Lockheed-Martin's LLV, CTA's ORBEX, and PacAstro Corporation's PA-2.

The U.S. can compete in the international market, but without trade agreements with economies-in-transition competition with foreign competitors becomes difficult. This is largely due to the fact that government subsidization tends to permit foreign competitors to price significantly lower than U.S. launch companies.

*Question III.b.* How would you evaluate the U.S. industry relative to its major competitors?

Answer. The U.S. industry offers the widest selection of launch vehicles in the medium/heavy class as well as the small vehicle class compared to its foreign competitors. For example, the Delta and Atlas vehicles have a performance capability range of 5,000 to 8,200 pounds to geosynchronous transfer orbit (GTO). There are currently 9 classes of U.S. small launch vehicles that have a lift capacity up to and including 5,000 pounds to LEO.

At present, the U.S. industry is undertaking research to develop new reusable launch vehicle technologies. Research and development roadmaps of some U.S. firms includes extensive, robust RLV technology maturation and demonstration programs. Improved technologies also affords the U.S. an advantage in launch site operations and customer satisfaction relative to economies in transition.

*Question III.c.* What strategies must the U.S. commercial launch industry pursue in order to enhance its competitiveness?

Answer. To be more competitive, the U.S. commercial launch industry must pursue the following:

• Support and sustain funding for launch system and infrastructure reliability improvements so as to reduce costs.

• Reduce industrial overhead in areas involving the launch system's operability.

• Aid in the streamlining of burdensome government regulatory procedures.

*Question IV.a.* What are your views regarding the recently negotiated U.S-China launch agreement which restricts the pricing and number of China's commercial launches?

Answer. Negotiating this agreement involved very close cooperation and consultation with all sectors of the commercial space industry including the satellite manufacturers, launch vehicle manufacturers, and service providers, in developing the terms and conditions.

On balance this agreement will provide greater market stability. It will also allow U.S. satellite manufacturers to have access to launch vehicles from China and supply satellites in that region of the world where there is an increased demand for satellite service.

It does not severely impact the U.S. launch vehicle manufacturers but strikes a balance between conflicting demands and needs of the satellite manufacturers and service providers and launch vehicle manufacturers and launch service providers.

*Question IV.b.* Why is the launch agreement more favorable to China than the earlier U.S.-Russian launch deal was favorable to Russia?

Answer. Although there may appear to be inequalities, when all the payloads and grandfathered launches are considered, the agreements are very comparable. For example, the Russian Agreement allows the launch of eight principal payloads, but four of those launches may have two satellites on a single rocket for a total of 12 payloads over a seven year period. This compares with 11 launches permitted in the China Agreement over a comparable seven year period. Each agreement also has a grandfather clause permitting four launches for Russia and four for China. Thus, the two agreements allow essentially equivalent access to the international launch market for equal periods of time.

In the low-earth-orbit market, the U.S. would have a concern only if China and other "economy-in-transition" launch service providers together exceed the share that western market suppliers will have. We have stipulated key factors that would be considered: for example, whether or not there was available launch supply from the West, and whether or not there were key business decisions. The intent was to not overly burden industry, and to provide industry with some guiding parameters to let them make the most informed business decisions.

With respect to pricing, we have a better understanding of the factors which lead to additional costs of doing business with China, compared to the U.S. or Europeans, and devising the relevant pricing provisions accordingly.

*Question IV.c.* Do you believe that the two agreements should be brought into conformity?

Answer. As noted above, we believe the agreements are comparable. However, the first request from the Russian Government to discuss the space launch trade agreement has just been received by USTR. No formal date for discussions has been set.

*Question IV.d.* Do we really need these agreements when the launch services are marketed as much on reliability as pricing?

Answer. The agreements are needed to assure a stable and orderly marketplace in which U.S. industry can compete on a fair and equitable basis.

With respect to reliability versus price in marketing efforts, Chinese and Russian marketing practices and discussions with payload owners indicate that pricing is still the dominant factor in selecting a launch services provider.

*Question IV.e.* Did the recent explosion of a Chinese rocket—which killed 6 people and injured 23—have any impact on its launch industry?

Answer. The recent explosion of the Long March 2E (LM-2E) in the attempted launch of the Asia-Pacific 2 satellite (AsiaSat 2) has had short term effects. Insurance rates have increased modestly and some payload providers have expressed nervousness about Chinese reliability. For example, trade press reports suggest that AsiaSat owners might reconsider replacement launch plans on another LM-2E, depending on.results of the launch failure investigation. However, the China Great Wall Industry Corporation still has a substantial backlog of orders, none of which has yet been canceled. China has remained a significant player in the contract competitions occurring after the failure.

*Question V.a.* Your office is years overdue in proposing regulations on insurance requirements for launch companies. Would you describe what the regulations would do and when your office plans to publish proposed regulations?

Answer. OCST intends to provide clarification and guidance to industry by establishing standardized procedures for implementing financial responsibility requirements and allocating risks. Currently, the Office plans to update and publish these requirements by the fourth quarter of fiscal year 1995. As a result, a notice of proposed rule making (NPRM) is being prepared, which is expected to lead to publication of a final rule late in the calendar year or early 1996.

Under the 1988 Amendments to the Commercial Space Launch Act, recodified at 49 U.S.C. Subtitle IX, ch. 701, persons authorized to conduct commercial launch activities under a license must obtain insurance (or otherwise demonstrate financial responsibility) to protect against third-party liability and Government property damage claims resulting from licensed activities. The Government must also be protected, through insurance or other assurances of financial responsibility, when its property or personnel are involved in commercial launch activities. OCST is responsible for setting insurance requirements according to a risk-based determination of the maximum probable loss that would result from licensed activities, up to a statutory ceiling of $500 million for third-party liability insurance and $100 million for Government property insurance. In addition, launch participants are required-to enter into reciprocal waivers of claims whereby each party agrees, among other things, to absorb certain losses it sustains as a result of licensed activities.

Currently, OCST prescribes insurance requirements for licensees on a case-by-case basis after analyzing the maximum probable third-party and government property losses associated with a launch proposal. Those requirements are imposed on licensees in license orders, as is the requirement to execute an interparty waiver of claims agreement. OCST monitors compliance by licensees with requirements on an on-going basis.

Through rulemaking, OCST intends to provide clarification and guidance to industry by establishing standardized procedures wherever practicable for implementing financial responsibility requirements and allocating risks.

In addition, OCST intends to utilize the rulemaking process to address a variety of issues associated with the statutory financial responsibility and allocation of risk regime. Concerns have arisen over the extent to which pre-launch activities are intended to be covered by statutorily-based financial responsibility requirements and the Government payment of excess third-party claims provisions. At the DOT-sponsored public meeting held in October 1994, OCST sought industry views on the kinds of criteria that may be used to determine whether and when an activity would be subject to statutory financial responsibility requirements and when payment by the U.S. Government of excess third-party claims may be available under the statute. OCST also sought views on how this regime would apply to licensed spaceport operators.

This additional guidance to industry1 and new ventures in particular, will allow industry to manage risks appropriately. It is increasingly important for untested technologies, such as reusable launch vehicles.

*Question V.b.* Given that the U.S. launch industry has operated without these regulations, do you believe they are really necessary?

Answer. These regulations will allow industry to manage risks appropriately, particularly in the area of new ventures. Regulations on insurance requirements are increasingly important for innovative companies entering the commercial launch industry with new, untested technologies, such as reusable launch vehicles.

*Question VI.a.* What is your view about NASA's program aimed at eventually developing a replacement for the Shuttle?

Answer. Development by NASA of a reusable launch vehicle (RLV) to replace the Shuttle appears to offer the potential for significantly reducing the cost of access to space in the long-term. It is imperative that NASA's plan and requirements provide opportunities for the private sector to develop commercial versions that can be operational to meet market needs by the turn of the century.

*Question VI.b.* What impact would a new Shuttle vehicle have on our commercial launch industry?

Answer. A new RLV begins to address a critical need for decreasing cost of access to space. The destruction of multi-million dollar ELVs after a single launch adds tremendously to the cost of access to space. The future of the U.S. launch industry and satellite production depends on reliable, economic access to space. The U.S. launch industry must lower the cost of access to space if it is to be competitive in the 21st century world market.

*Question VI.c.* Do you believe we should look at "privatizing" the current Shuttle program?

Answer. NASA is looking at a broad range of options as part of their overall agency reinvention process, including privatization issues. They are investigating and consolidating recommendations from numerous internal and external reviews that will be reflected in the President's FY 1997 Budget.

*Question VI.d.* What would be the advantages and disadvantages of privatizing the Shuttle?

Answer. Presumably, achieving lower cost while maintaining system reliability and operability would be significant incentives for varying levels of privatization. There remain, however, potential concerns regarding the ability of a commercial entity to ensure public safety and reliability during Shuttle launches, raising the issue of the need for regulatory oversight. The issue of sustaining an adequate level of R&D for system improvements and maintenance must also be addressed.

It should be borne in mind that full privatization suggests a contractor would operate the Shuttle program on a "for-profit" basis. However, the Government is presently the only Shuttle customer. One can assume such an arrangement would result in increased costs to the Government since the commercial operator would have to bear all the operations expenses the Government presently bears, in addition to profit-margin. The principal difference between a public and private entity is that the former acts in the general public interest, and the latter acts in the interest of private investors. The Government would not be in a position to purchase these launch services on a competitive basis and, accordingly, higher costs to the Government could be a likely disadvantage of such a course.

National Aeronautics and
Space Administration

**Office of the Administrator**
Washington, DC  20546-0001

APR 2 1 1995


The Honorable Conrad Burns
Chairman
Subcommittee on Science, Technology
    and Space
Committee on Commerce, Science
    and Transportation
United States Senate
Washington, DC   20510


Dear Mr. Chairman:

     During my March 1, 1995, testimony before the Subcommittee
concerning NASA's FY 1996 budget request, we discussed Russian
participation in the international Space Station and NASA's
contingency planning in the event that Russia's involvement
were severely curtailed or terminated.   I would like to
elaborate upon NASA's contingency planning for the record.

     First, the decision to invite Russia to participate in
the international Space Station allows NASA to benefit from
the considerable knowledge and expertise which the Russian
space program has acquired from many years in long-duration
space flight.   Second, inclusion of the Russians has been
estimated to save the United States approximately $2 billion in
costs associated with elements that Russia will provide and to
enable completion of Station assembly approximately 15 months
earlier.   Russian participation allows the Station to be
serviced from a variety of launch vehicles, in addition to the
Space Shuttle, providing greater access to the Station.
Finally, inclusion of one of the world's major spacefaring
nations in this endeavor makes the international Space Station
truly a historical and global effort that will demonstrate what
great things can be accomplished through partnerships whose
objective is a common good.

     It is NASA's intent that, if Russia were unwilling or
unable to continue participation in the international Space
Station--at whatever stage or for whatever reason--we would
complete assembly of the Space Station with our other partners.
In the unlikely event that Russia were to withdraw its
participation, NASA has planned for two general scenarios:

1.  A complete withdrawal by the Russian government, but continued participation in the program on the part of Russian manufacturers, who would be available as contractors.

2.  A total withdrawal of Russia from the program, including Russian industrial concerns.

Under the first scenario, NASA would continue along the present design path and negotiate acquisition of hardware directly from the Russian manufacturers. NASA would continue with plans to procure the Russian Functional Cargo Block (FGB) from the manufacturer, Khrunichev, according to the existing schedule. Under the second scenario, NASA would activate its contingency plans to cover life support and crew-rescue functions. These plans call for the United States to provide redundancy for all critical life-support systems. For example, NASA would provide a second oxygen generation capability. Regarding crew-rescue capability, NASA would postpone early permanent crew habitation until the planned Crew Rescue Vehicle becomes available. NASA would establish a U.S. crew rescue option and a plan for propellant resupply and reboost capabilities with the European Space Agency.

The most critical requirement under the second scenario would be provision of a functionally equivalent replacement for the FGB and the combination of Russian assets which support it. The FGB is the first building block element of the Station. It is an active, self-sufficient, orbiting spacecraft with electrical power generation, attitude control, propulsion, guidance, navigation, communication, and thermal-control capabilities. Contingency planning to reduce the risk associated with dependence upon Russia for provision of the FGB was initiated early in the program. One aspect of that planning was implemented on February 6, 1995, with the reaching of an agreement between Lockheed and Khrunichev to procure the FGB.

Further review of the contingency plan for a total Russian default scenario (including default on the FGB) is under way within the Space Station program. Early fall-back plans are being reviewed to minimize impacts upon current Station hardware designs, assembly sequence, and schedule. Several options are under consideration, and selection of the optimum approach is expected to be completed by this summer.

It is clearly in the interest of the United States for Russia to participate as a full partner. A complete pull out by Russia would be manifested in terms of higher costs for the United States and a severe impact on the schedule. It is Russian participation that makes it possible for NASA to complete the program under a $2.1 billion annual cap and to complete assembly of the international Space Station--with all of its capability for conduct of on-orbit scientific research and technology--by FY 2002.

    I would be pleased to discuss this matter with you in greater detail, if you wish.

Sincerely,

Daniel S. Goldin
Administrator

cc:
The Honorable John D. Rockefeller, IV

Responses to written questions submitted by Chrm. Pressler resulting from the March 12, 1995, hearing.

Question 1: Completion of Space Station assembly is now scheduled for the year 2002. However, when the previous program was first begun in 1984, completion was promised by 1992 -- three years ago! What is the reason for these chronic schedule slippages and what assurances can you give Congress that it will not continue?

Answer 1: Program delays since 1984 have largely been the result of redirection from either the Congress or the Administration in either the scope or content of the space station program. (See Attachment A)

In addition to mandated changes in the program, and responses to ever-increasing budget pressures, there were duplications and inefficiencies in NASA's space station management during the Freedom period, from 1984 to 1992. After the 1992 election, President Clinton, in March of 1993, directed NASA to review the space station and propose a means of building it faster, better, and cheaper. The result of that review and the independent Presidential advisory commission headed by Dr. Charles Vest, President of MIT, was the Alpha station configuration announced in September of 1993.

At the same time, changes were being made in the management and contracting concepts for the Space Station program. Duplicative management levels were eliminated and multiple prime contracts were re-scoped to a single prime contractor. It was announced in August, 1993, that Johnson Space Center would be the single host center for the space station program office, which would report directly to a Program Director at NASA headquarters. In November, the Russians were invited to participate in the program, and the station configuration was subsequently modified to reflect the use of their equipment and capabilities.

Since all of these activities have taken place, the Program Office and the Prime Contractor, Boeing Defense and Space Group, have continued to refine the details of the space station configuration. Recently, the Program conducted the first Incremental Design Review, which both signifies and documents that the program is on track with a design that will fly and perform as advertised.

Question 2: Mr. Goldin, the Alpha program needs 45 launches to get to assembly complete. Twenty-seven of those launches are Shuttle launches; 16 are Russian launches, and 2 are supplied by the Europeans. By contrast, the old Freedom program required a total of only about 28 Shuttle launches.

Would you agree that the Alpha program is inherently more complex than Freedom as a result of the additional required flights?

Answer 2: It is true that the international Space Station appears more complex than the previous design -- however, any added complexity is due to the larger size and increased capabilities of the Station. The addition of Russia as an international partner added capabilities such as more volume, more power, more crew, and more laboratory modules to the Space Station.

The international Space Station is a much more robust space station. It is larger

92

and involves more components, but also more inherent capabilities and functions that Freedom never would have had, in terms of research capability. Of the 27 Shuttle missions scheduled in support of the station, 21 are dedicated for assembly, comparable to Freedom. The remaining six flights are dedicated utilization missions to the Space Station.

As you pointed out, almost all of the additional flights are to launch Russian elements. Additionally, the experience gained during non-U.S. flights will increase our ability to rely on vehicles other than the Shuttle for access to the Space Station.

Question 3: Mr. Goldin, it was originally claimed that Russian participation would save the Space Station program $2 billion. As you know, last June, the General Accounting Office disagreed. In fact, the GAO concluded that Russian involvement could result in "little or no net savings." What is NASA's most recent assessment of the impact of Russian involvement on Space Station costs?

Answer 3: NASA maintains that Russian participation in the international Space Station Program will produce a net savings of at least $2.0 billion. The differences between the savings identified by NASA and the costs estimated by the GAO report rests primarily in GAO's failure to consider the savings incurred by assembly complete occurring fifteen months earlier and NASA's ability to provide propulsion/reboost capability and crew rescue capability within its budget cap of $2.1 billion.

Since the GAO published their report last year, the program has met several significant milestones that contribute to the program's ability to complete the Station on time and on budget. First, extensive fact finding activities were carried out with Boeing and each of the first tier subcontractors. Adjustments were made in program content and the development approach, followed by contract negotiations with Boeing prime. A final contract was signed on January 13, 1995. Second, similar fact finding activities were performed in the operations areas and the resulting efficiencies have been incorporated. Third, we entered into a contract with Lockheed for the procurement of the Russian-built FGB. Fourth, we have just completed a successful design review which verified that the program is on track for assembly complete in June 2002 - consistent with NASA's estimated savings for accelerated assembly. These events, combined with the impressive operational, hardware and design milestones being met by the program, places us squarely on schedule and on budget to deliver a station with greater user capabilities, more power and a larger crew size than the previous design.

Question 3a: Last week, top Russian space officials warned that their space program is near collapse. Further, they threatened to evacuate cosmonauts from Mir and cancel all international space contracts unless funding for their space projects is increased. Would you share with the Subcommittee any details about this disturbing development? What impact will it have on the Space Station program? Will this give more ammunition to Station critics who believe it suffers from over reliance on the Russians?

Answer 3a: The Russian Space Agency (RSA) has been largely successful in its request for increases in its budget. It is now expected that the Russian government will transfer funds from Russia's science budget to assist with the funding of science missions that RSA oversees. In doing so, RSA will be able to spend most of its budget on human spaceflight, including cooperative programs with the U.S.

The Russian space program and its associated launch infrastructure is one of the most experienced and successful programs in the world. In 1994, the Russian Military Space Forces, which manages the Russian launch infrastructure, carried out 49 launches and delivered 64 satellites into space. Additionally, three manned Soyuz TM spacecraft and five Progress M freighters were launched to support the work on the Mir station. Recent Russian press accounts suggests that launches will increase in 1995 and that the approved space budget will be satisfactory to support operations.

The current international Space Station plan, as agreed to by the U.S., Japan, Canada, and the member nations of the European Space Agency, doesn't contain an over reliance on any of our international partners. A partnership, by nature, establishes a framework for each member of the partnership to contribute something unique in support of common objectives. Russian participation provides increased access, expanded capability for earth observation, increased research capability, full life support redundancy, earlier completion of the station assembly, and enhanced orbital maintenance capability, not to mention a wealth of experience in long-duration space flight.

Due to continual pressure to reduce program cost, the 1993 Space Station redesign sought to take advantage of the proven capabilities that Russian flight hardware and infrastructure have to offer. The resulting design was approved by the Congress in 1994 . Should Russia withdraw from the program for any reason, the impact would depend greatly upon timing, and how far along the program is in assembly. Another variable is whether Russian contractors would continue to participate, even in the absence of Russian government participation--as in the case of acquisition of the Functional Energy Block (FGB), for example. Estimates showed that the addition of Russia to the project saved $2 billion and shortened assembly time by 15 months. As a general rule, the absence of Russian participation would--all or in part--negate those savings. We have ongoing analysis and contingency plans to minimize adverse program impacts should that occur, and to keep the program on track.

Question 4: Mr. Goldin, the Alpha plan calls for Space Station to fly at an Orbit inclination of 51.6 degrees to permit access by Russian rockets. While it facilitates Russian access, it reduces the payload capacity and launch "windows" for the Shuttle flights to Space Station. If the Russians have to pull out of the Space Station for any reason, do you disagree that the higher inclination will place the U.S. at a disadvantage?

Answer 4: The 51.6 inclination was recommended by the Vest committee and is an orbit that all partners can achieve, while retaining the ability to carry crew and cargo. It provides the Station with multiple-vehicle access, reduces the dependence upon the Shuttle, and offers greater Earth coverage while not creating safety issues concerning launches over populated areas. To achieve the higher performance required of the 51.6 inclination, the Space Station program will use the planned permanent performance improvements being made to the Shuttle fleet. Any decision to lower the Station's orbit would be dependent upon the time of the Russian withdrawal, the status of the Shuttle improvements and the desires of the science community.

Question 5: Does NASA have any plans in the future to use Space Station as a stopover base for manned missions to the Moon? Does the current Space Station design permit the facility to be used as a transportation node for lunar visits? If not, what changes in the design would have to be made?

Answer 5: Current plans of the Agency and the international Space Station do not include a role in a human lunar mission. However, the modular design of the Space Station allows it to expand, provided the funding is available. Several considerations would have to be made if such an expansion were undertaken, including operational changes, flight scheduling, and the impact on the microgravity research environment

Question 6: Mr. Goldin, Space Station Freedom was designed to have a lifetime of about 30 years. Space Station Alpha is being designed to have an on-orbit lifetime of only 15 years - - half the lifetime of the previous program. Moreover, five of those fifteen years will be for Alpha's construction, leaving an actual operational lifetime of only ten years. Would you explain why a Space Station offering half the lifetime of the previous design is a better buy for the American people?

Answer 6: A significant factor in the cost of the previous Space Station design was the unprecedented, 30-year lifetime requirement. In order to reduce the cost of the current international Space Station design and its yearly operational cost, the minimum lifetime requirement was reduced. However, we expect the actual lifetime capability of the international Space Station to be longer than the minimum requirement.

The international Space Station is larger and more capable than the previous Alpha design, and costs $2 billion less, so it clearly is a better deal. As compared to the Freedom program, the international Space Station program is more realistically priced, and the design is more mature and supportable. In addition, over 75% of the planned Freedom hardware and software capabilities have been incorporated into the international Space Station.

Question 7: Mr. Goldin, have any stability analyses of Space Station Alpha been undertaken? What happens if, for example, a Shuttle orbiter or a Russian vehicle docks too violently with Alpha? This problem has occurred in the past during Russian dockings with their Mir" space station. What is the risk of structural damage or disruption of scientific experiments from violent dockings?

Answer 7: Load analyses have been done on each element of the International Space Station, and have been reviewed in the context of the load factors of Russians elements and the timing and nature of docking contacts throughout the assembly and operation of the station. There is no critical concern about maintaining the structural integrity of the station or of remaining within the bounds of crew safety requirements.

With respect to scientific experiment disruption, two major initiatives address that question: first, vibro-acoustic isolation and minimization of impact of contacts; and secondly, mission operations planning and scheduling of quiet microgravity periods, versus periods of rendezvous, resupply and associated activity.

Question 8. Mr. Goldin, as I understand the current Space Station program, there are no hardware backups. If, for example, a piece of Station hardware is lost during launch to Space Station, or while on orbit during assembly, massive program dislocations would result. Is this true, and if so, does it constitute a fundamental weakness for the program?

Answer 8: It must be recognized that the international Space Station is the most challenging project ever attempted in terms of the large number of elements that must be coordinated on the ground and assembled on orbit. It is also a fact that it would not be economically feasible to build spare hardware as replacements for each launch package, and was never a part of any previous configuration. We are currently assessing impacts and options at each stage, or launch, of space station hardware. We are looking at the impacts of 1) delay of launch, 2) loss of launch package and 3) loss of launch package and launch vehicle (including the loss of an orbiter). Our preliminary analysis reflects no single incident that would prevent the final assembly and successful operation of a space station. In some cases, on-orbit science and utilization is slightly decreased, but in all cases a successful on-orbit science platform is achieved. This is due to the modularity and redundancy in the space station design. The complexity and cost of dealing with each contingency would depend on the time of occurrence of the loss and the specific payload in question. We remain confident in our ability to successfully complete the goal of deploying an effective station with robust science capability.

Although risk will always be a part of space flight, the more practical approach to increasing the Space Station program's success is to pursue higher reliability in both Shuttle launches and Station assembly operations through hardware upgrades, extensive crew training, and acquisition of operational experience through the Shuttle-Mir missions.

Question 9: It is my understanding that, in the assembly of Space Station Alpha, there is little or no room for any errors or failures. And yet, it is going to require 45 flights to get to assembly complete, with each and every launch required in sequence to be successful, not to mention each and every on-orbit assembly sequence. Has anybody at NASA computed the probability of being able to accomplish this, and if so, what are the results of the study?

Answer 9: As stated in response to the previous question, it is not true that the flights needed for Space Station assembly require a certain sequence, due to the modularity of the station design. There are some limiting factors, based primarily on issues like power requirements and life support capabilities, but these would have the impact of scheduling on-orbit activities differently, more than anything else.

The reliability of the launch vehicles involved is very high. There are currently 21 Space Shuttle flights required for the assembly of the Space Station, and the Space Shuttle Program has a reliability of over 98.5%. There have been many operational and processing improvements incorporated into the Space Shuttle Program to reduce the incidence of launch delays and cancellations. A total probability/risk model is in development for the entire space station assembly and operation, but is not yet complete. The results will be briefed to the Congress when they become available.

Question 10: Mr. Goldin, will it be possible to add on any new modules to Alpha in the years after 2002? If so, how would you accomplish it? Would it be relatively easy? Could a module dedicated to remote sensing activities be added to Space Station?

Answer 10: If funding were available, the modular design of the international Space Station would allow for expansion of its current capabilities or the addition of new capabilities. As stated in the previous question on a lunar mission, other aspects of the Space Station operations and science would have to be considered prior to any expansion. A module dedicated to remote sensing could be among the expanded capabilities, again dependent on available funding and Agency priorities.

Question 11: Space Station is devoted mainly to microgravity and life sciences research. Why was remote sensing not included as one of the core functions of Space Station Alpha? Is it true that remote sensing capability was one of the major reasons given for moving Alpha to the 51.6 degree inclination?

Answer 11: Remote sensing is among the capabilities of the international Space Station. However, other programs within NASA (such Mission to Planet Earth) and elsewhere provide a greater capability for remote sensing. The decision to move to a 51.6 degree inclination was due in part to the greater Earth coverage, but the key consideration was the inclusion of Russia as an international partner and the access of all international partners' launch vehicles to the new inclination. An external payload for MTPE, SAGE III, is planned for the station.

Question 11a: Several weeks ago, it was reported that France and Germany want to cut in half the European Space Agency's contribution. If that occurs, what would be its impact on the Space Station program?

Answer 11a: At its March 23 meeting, the ESA Council reaffirmed Europe's determination to be an active partner in the international Space Station, and ESA Director General Luton expressed his confidence that sufficient progress is being made to finalize Europe's commitment to the program and to bring the decision process to a successful conclusion: a major role for Europe in the international Space Station.

The ESA council also confirmed ESA's contribution to the program: the Columbus Orbital Facility, a multidisciplinary utilization program, and the Ariane-5/ATV. A final decision on the European contribution will be taken at the October 18-20, 1995, ESA Ministerial meeting.

However, if any member nations of ESA decide to reduce funding for the Space Station, the effect would be determined by the size of the cut and the specific elements or contributions that would be reduced or eliminated. Significant cuts in ESA funding could result in launch delays, which could affect our utilization plans, as we currently have rights to approximately half of the European laboratory. However, ESA funding reductions would not affect the ability of the U.S. and its other partners to proceed with the program.

Question 12: I believe that all NASA programs should strive to be relevant to the taxpayers that pay for them. With that in mind, would you share with us examples of how Mission to Planet Earth will benefit Plains States like South Dakota, particularly in terms of the agricultural community? What are your thoughts about proposals to distribute the land data at the EROS Data Center to benefit farmers, researchers, students, and land-use planners throughout South Dakota and other Plains States?

Answer 12: In addition to the basic science and research conducted by the Office of Mission To Planet Earth (MTPE), several programs are under way to bring the benefits of research and use of NASA's satellite data to the state and local level. One example of this is a project to utilize space-based remote sensing to provide information to the agricultural community on specific crop types, and aquifer use rates with resulting water availability. Additionally, MTPE's work on climate modeling and prediction will lead to greater accuracy in long term weather forecasting, which will be of great benefit to the agriculture community. In fact, NASA has established it's first cooperative arrangement with a local TV weather station to utilize NASA's data available over the Internet as part of their daily broadcasts. MTPE is also involved in investigation of techniques utilizing remote sensing for emergency management including such things as flood planning, mitigation and emergency response.

In addition to these specific projects, MTPE is developing an infrastructure through the Earth Observing System Data and Information System (EOSDIS) to make Earth science information more accessible to the public. For instance, the Earth Resources Observation System (EROS) Data Center in Sioux Falls, South Dakota provides users with land processes imagery that has the potential to be translated into valuable applications. We are encouraging private industry and state/local governments to transform this basic Earth science information available from EROS and other NASA DAACs into value added products that meet the needs of their defined user community. In the Plains states such as the Dakotas, this data will be especially useful for farmers and ranchers. This undertaking by NASA and other federal agencies is part of an overall effort to examine the best way to establish government, academic, and commercial partnerships to extend the utilization of EOSDIS to non-research user communities such as education, agriculture, state and local planning, adjudication, transportation, and emergency management.

Question 13a: EOSDIS - the data collection component of Mission to Planet Earth - probably represents the biggest challenge in the program. Are you confident that EOSDIS will be able to handle the enormous amounts of data the climate change satellite will generate?

Answer 13a: Yes. We are confident existing and expected technologies are capable of supporting EOSDIS requirements. Through an incremental development approach, EOSDIS will be able to handle the data generated by the MTPE satellites as each mission is launched. EOSDIS development is already proceeding to support the first launch. The prototype version of the system (Version 0) is already giving us valuable experience which we will use to improve future versions. And there is much more to come. We have designed the system to be flexible and evolvable. Specifically, we have sized the ground stations and data production facilities to receive and process all data received from all EOS satellites; the internal networks have sufficient bandwidth to transfer this data to the DAACs for permanent archive; and the DAACs have sufficient processing and archive capacity to transform the raw data into useful products. When completed, EOSDIS will be the largest civilian data system ever devised by the U.S. Government.

In addition to using technologies that exist today, EOSDIS will take appropriate advantage of technological advances as they occur in the future, through the use of just-in-time procurements, an open system architecture, prototyping, modular design, and other features. Woven into the EOSDIS design is the ability to adapt to increases in the amount and rate of raw data input, a larger and changing user community, and an evolution in data and product requirements. Confidence in EOSDIS also comes from the community beyond NASA, including the National Research Council and the EOSDIS Advisory Panel, which have both endorsed the current approach.

Question 13b: What will be the main types of data collected by EOSDIS and what will it be used for?

Answer 13b: The EOSDIS data will be used to conduct the first comprehensive study of interaction between atmosphere, oceans, land and life on Earth, which is central to understanding climate. These data will enable reseachers from all over the world to measure phenomena such as cloud formation and precipitation, changes in forests, deserts, crop land and rivers, and the movement of energy, water and gases through the atmosphere and oceans leading to floods, droughts and other climate changes. Other measurements will detect changes in glaciers and polar ice sheets affecting sea level and global fresh water balance, and the effects of the sun, wind, volcanoes, ozone, and life in the oceans on changes in weather patterns and climate. In the years ahead, we hope to understand the global and regional climate changes occuring on Earth, and distinguish between natural changes and those influenced by human activities.

Each Mission to Planet Earth instrument or satellite has a specific focus: oceans, atmosphere, land and life. The DAACs will process the data from each instrument into several products, and scientists will compare and combine these products to better understand the Earth from a regional and global perspective. These data will increase scientific understanding of the Earth as an integrated environmental system and its vulnerability to natural variations and human influences. EOSDIS data will also serve as the basis for numerous other applications, such as precision weather forecasting one to two weeks in advance, predicting seasonal trends such as droughts and floods, land use management, crop assessment, improving fishermen's catch, and educational tools for our youth. We hope that by making our data easily accessible and useful, we will encourage the private sector to invest in transforming scientific information into marketable products.

99

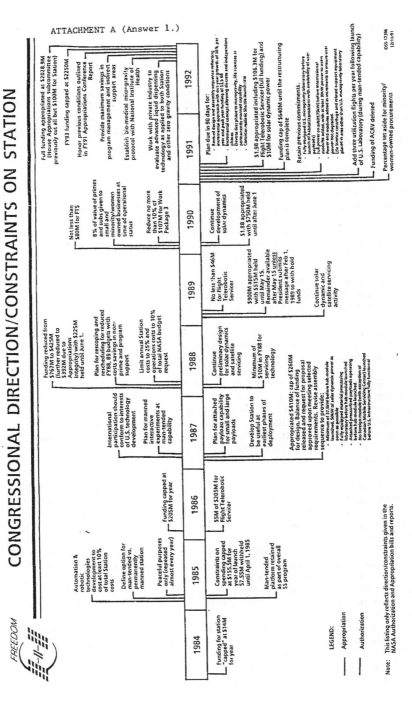

# CONGRESSIONAL DIRECTION/CONSTRAINTS ON STATION

Responses to written questions submitted by Chrm. Burns resulting from the March 1, 1995, hearing.

NASA Budget

Question 1: NASA's five year plan calls for reducing annual funding from $14.3 billion in FY 96 to $13.2 billion in FY 2000. This is $18 billion less than the five year profile assumed in the FY 1994 request and $5 billion less than the profile assumed in the FY 1995 request. How can NASA achieve those dramatic budget cuts and still continue current programs?

Answer 1: NASA is in the process of examining how the reduction included in the FY 1996 NASA request can be accommodated through reductions in NASA's overall institution. A team is in the midst of conducting a zero-base manpower review to plan these reductions. Programs will be considered for reduction only if the needed reductions cannot be taken through restructuring. The dramatic changes needed to transform NASA into a more efficient, smaller organization will allow the agency to focus on cutting edge research and technology within a smaller budget envelope.

Question 2: In the five-year plan, almost $4 billion of the cuts are characterized as "resolved percentage reductions". How and when does NASA plan to address these "unresolved" reductions.

Answer 2: Several teams are reviewing activities underway at NASA, and decisions concerning any restructuring at NASA will be made as part of the FY 1997 budget process.

Question 3: NASA has indicated that the budget reduction effort will give preference to programs over people. In your view, what will that entail? How much does NASA intend to cut personnel and will the personnel reductions emphasize buyouts or layoffs? What steps is NASA taking to insure that, in cutting jobs, it does not lose older workers with critical skills and experiences? If NASA were to lose critical personnel, is NASA's workforce such that qualified younger workers could step in to fill the void?

Answer 3: The NASA budget is cut by billions, jobs have to be impacted. The jobs may be those of our contractors or our own civil service employees. We have been reducing contractors in the Shuttle program and gaining efficiencies. When we restructured the Space Station last year, we eliminated 1000 civil service jobs through a buyout. Those cuts were necessary. Now our budget run outs are such that we must look harder at contractor and civil service jobs to eliminate the unnecessary, cut out duplication, and focus the workforce even more finely on our programs. Rather than saying we will give preference to programs over people, it would be more accurate to say that the preference is for programs over infrastructure. We have reviews underway to determine just what infrastructure is needed to enable the programs to operate efficiently. Excess infrastructure in the form of people, facilities, and buildings, has to be identified and shed. I expect to have the information I need by mid May in order to make planning decisions for the FY 1997 budget. When I came to the Agency in 1992, we were busy building an infrastructure suitable for a $30 billion budget. Now, we cannot afford such an infrastructure on what we expect to get.

In reducing our civil service workforce, we have certainly emphasized buyouts over layoffs. We had a buyout in 1994 that allowed over 1100 employees to leave voluntarily. The buyout we have underway now will end on March 31, 1995. We anticipate that an additional 1500 or more employees will leave. Most of those who take a buyout are older workers who have a wealth of experience. We have a tremendously talented cadre of younger workers who I am confident can get the job done. We have extended the buyout departure date for a few persons who are needed to finish critical work.

NASA will need to make additional workforce reductions after the buyout option is no longer available. While we will attempt to avoid the use of involuntary methods of separations such as reductions-in-force, RIFs at some NASA sites may prove unavoidable. We continue to look for other tools that may be used to encourage more voluntary separations. NASA may find it necessary to approach the Administration and Congress in order to obtain legislation to give the Agency flexibility to use such tools.

Question 4. Many have said that meaningful cost reduction at NASA will ultimately require eliminating or consolidating some of NASA ⌐s 12 Field Centers However, it has been reported that a NASA "white paper" calls for a radical reorganization of the Centers but stops short of recommending closings. Is NASA actively considering some kind of restructuring of the Field Centers? If some NASA Centers do have to be closed, what kind of process would be used to select the Centers to be closed? How would you compare the problems associated with closing NASA Centers with those involved in closing U.S. military bases?

Answer 4: Current federal budget realities are forcing major changes in the way government agencies conduct their missions. NASA has been at the forefront of change; NASA ⌐s goal is to continue providing high return to U.S. taxpayers in an era of declining budgets. NASA is undergoing a series of reviews aimed at effecting a major restructuring to meet this goal. Everything is on the table, including realignment of Center roles and missions and possible closure of some facilities and secondary sites. The results of the reviews are expected in mid-May and will be used as part of the development of the FY 1997 budget. Any proposed restructuring efforts will follow NASA ⌐s established countdown procedure that includes coordination with offices in the White House, OSTP, OMB, other Federal agencies, Congress, unions, and our customers and contractors. With only nine Centers and one Laboratory, the problems with closing NASA Centers would be the same as those involved in closing U.S. military bases but would have a proportionately much greater impact on NASA and its programs.

Question 4a: That NASA "white paper" also recommends that NASA explore the possibility of each Center being managed by a university, as is the case at NASA's Jet Propulsion Lab (which is managed by Cal Tech). What are the advantages and disadvantages of the Jet Propulsion Lab model, particularly with respect to costs and efficiency?

Answer 4a: Transferring existing NASA Centers and workforces to the private sector with university management would be done for quality and effectiveness reasons rather than cost benefits. Freedom from civil service regulations on compensation, personnel practices, financial disclosure, and post-employment would enable recruitment and retention of the best scientific, engineering, and managerial talent in the nation. An issue that would need to be resolved would be the transportability or continuity of civil service retirement benefits. The possibility of additional use of the JPL model will be considered in the NASA reinvention process.

Question 5. To reduce NASA ғs bureaucracy, some have argued that NASA should concentrate on cutting-edge research and development and leave operational space activities to the private sector. Some have even suggested "privatizing" some NASA programs like the Space Shuttle. What is your reaction to this viewpoint?

What should NASA ғs core mission be? What are some of the NASA programs that might be more cost-effectively performed by the private sector?

Answer 5: Over time, space operations has taken a larger portion of the NASA budget. NASA currently is undergoing a series of reviews in order to effect a major restructuring in light of budget realities and to reemphasize its role as leader of research and development. In the course of these reviews, we will be making decisions that will lead to fundamental changes in the way NASA conducts its mission. NASA ғs mission is to explore, use and enable the development of space for human enterprise; to advance scientific knowledge and understanding of the Earth, the Solar System, and the Universe, and use the environment of space for research; and to research, develop, verify and transfer advanced aeronautics, space and related technologies. In this constrained budget environment, NASA simply cannot afford to do things the private sector is better equipped to do. As the reviews proceed, we will keep the Subcommittee informed of progress in identifying areas which may lend themselves to greater private sector involvement or outright privatization. We will also collaborate to better understand privatization and the several means for effecting it.

Space Station

Question 6: In recent years, the $30 billion Space Station has been redesigned; Russian participation has been added; and management has been consolidated. Has the look, content, cost, construction schedule, and management for Space Station finally been stabilized or will there be more changes in the future?

Answer 6: The current design of the international Space Station resulted from the 1993 redesign effort undertaken at the request of the White House. The redesign effort yielded a stable station design that provides more capabilities at a lower cost than the Freedom design, and the inclusion of Russia as an international partner provides a Station on orbit 15 months earlier than the previous design and significantly enhances research capabilities, such as increased power, crew, and volume. If funding for the international Space Station is stable, we are confident that we can meet our schedule and projected milestones.

After the appointment of the Program Manager and Program Director over a year ago, the program's management has stabilized. Contributing to the program's stability was the establishment of the Space Station Program Office at its Host

Center, Johnson Space Center; the selection of Boeing as the single Prime Contractor and the definitization of the Boeing/NASA contract. NASA and its contractor team members have structured the program management under an Integrated Product Team (IPT) concept, which is output, or product, focused. The Space Station Program has established an effective performance measurement system throughout the Program and continues to improve overall efficiency.

Question 7a. Russian involvement in Space Station has been defended in part on the basis of an estimated $2 billion in cost savings. However, last year, the General Accounting office said that Russian Participation would not save money. At this juncture, does NASA have a better sense of the costs and savings associated with the Russian participation?

Answer 7a: Since the GAO published their report last year, the program has met several significant milestones that contribute to the program's ability to complete the Station on time and on budget. First, extensive fact finding activities were carried out with Boeing and each of the first tier subcontractors. Adjustments were made in program content and the development approach, followed by contract negotiations with Boeing prime. A final contract was signed on January 13, 1995. Second, similar fact finding activities were performed in the operations areas and the resulting efficiencies have been incorporated. Third, we entered into a contract with Lockheed for the procurement of the Russian-built FGB. Fourth, we have just completed a successful design review which verified that the program is on track for assembly complete in June 2002 - consistent with NASA's estimated savings for accelerated assembly. These events, combined with the impressive operational, hardware and design milestones being met by the program, places us squarely on schedule and on budget to deliver a station with greater user capabilities, more power and a larger crew size than the previous design.

Question 7b: Under the most recent plan, what are the major elements of the Russian contribution to Space Station?

Answer 7b: See Attachment A for a summary of the Russian elements of the International Space Station.

Question 7c: In your view, does the current Space Station plan contain an over reliance on the Russian contribution?

Answer 7c: The current international Space Station plan, as agreed to by the U.S., Japan, Canada, and the member nations of the European Space Agency, doesn't contain an over reliance, but rather a necessary reliance on all of our international partners, not just the Russians. A partnership, by nature, establishes a framework for each member of the partnership to contribute something unique in support of common objectives. Russian participation provides increased access, expanded capability for earth observation, increased research capability, full life support redundancy, earlier completion of the station assembly, and enhanced orbital maintenance capability, not to mention a wealth of experience in long-duration space flight.

Due to continual pressure to reduce program cost, the 1993 Space Station redesign sought to take advantage of the proven capabilities that Russian flight hardware and infrastructure have to offer. The $2 billion savings resulting from the redesigned program was approved by the Congress in 1994.

Nonetheless, NASA policy indicates that if Russia is unwilling or unable to continue participation in the international Space Station, at whatever stage and for whatever reason, this will not prevent our completion of the Space Station with our other partners. In order to prepare for this unlikely eventuality, thorough and realistic contingency plans are under development which ensure the station's success even without the advantages of Russian participation.

It should be pointed out, however, that the loss of Russian participation would require additional U.S. funding to offset the loss of their full participation.

Question 7d: Aerospace Daily reported on February 27, 1995, that there is a near collapse in the Russian space program and that the funding for Mir is under threat. If this were to happen, would the Station still be able to remain on track with minimal cost to overruns or schedule slippage?

Answer 7d: The Russian Space Agency (RSA) has been largely successful in its request for increases in its budget. It is now expected that the Russian government will transfer funds from Russia's science budget to assist with the funding of science missions that RSA oversees. In doing so, RSA will be able to spend most of it budget on human spaceflight, including cooperative programs with the U.S.

Should Russia withdraw from the program for any reason, the impact would depend greatly upon timing and how far along the program is in assembly. Another variable is whether Russian contractors would continue to participate, in the absence of Russian government participation--as in the case of acquisition of the Functional Cargo Block (FGB), for example. Estimates showed that the addition of Russia to the project saved $2 billion and shortened assembly time by 15 months. As a general rule, the absence of Russian participation would--all or in part--negate those savings. We have developed contingency plans and are conducting continued analysis to minimize adverse program impacts should that occur.

Question 7e: How sound is the Russian launch infrastructure and space program? How does it compare to the U.S. space program and launch infrastructure?

Answer 7e: The Russian space program and its associated launch infrastructure is one of the most experienced and successful programs in the world. In 1994, the Russian Military Space Forces, which manages the Russian launch infrastructure, carried out 49 launches and delivered 64 satellites into space. Additionally, three manned Soyuz TM spacecraft and five Progress M freighters were launched to support work on the Mir station. Recent Russian press stories suggests that launches will increase in 1995 and that the approved space budget will be satisfactory to support operations. Those reports are consistent with our own understanding of Russia's space program status.

Question 7f: Is there any factual basis for concerns that the use of Russian hardware, launches, and personnel in the Space Station program will, in effect, transfer jobs from the U.S. to Russia?

Answer 7f: Including Russia in the international Space Station program does not transfer jobs from the Unites States. The Station redesign that occurred in 1993 was tasked to lower costs as its primary objective and NASA reduced both contractor and civil service employment in the Space Station Program in order to meet this objective. By including the Russian elements, the Program added back content and capability which would not have been included in the redesigned station.

Additionally, there are benefits for U.S. companies from Russian participation, since they are experiencing improved access to technologies and increased interaction (competitive contracting) between U.S. and Russian firms in a variety of aerospace technologies. This increases high-quality jobs and therefore is advantageous for both countries.

Question 8: Assuming the Russian space program stays intact over the next three years, beginning this June, NASA will fly seven Shuttle missions to the Russian space station Mir. What do you hope to accomplish through these Shuttle/Mir flights?

Answer 8: There are three primary objectives of the Shuttle-Mir program, known as Phase I of the international Space Station Program. The first key objective of the Shuttle-Mir program is to learn how to work with the Russians during joint missions, such as overcoming differences in language and culture and coordinating operations between the two control centers.

Second, NASA will gain valuable experience that will reduce the technical risks during construction and operation of the Station. Mir provides a unique opportunity to try out many techniques and solve problems before we construct our own Station. Additionally, the flights to Mir will enable the Shuttle program to better understand the 51.6 degree orbital inclination and its effects on Shuttle operations.

Finally, the Shuttle-Mir program will enable NASA to take advantage of Mir to provide early opportunities for extended scientific research. For example, U.S. astronaut Norm Thagard began a 90-day stay on Mir in March, and he is now conducting significant medical and life sciences research aboard Mir.

The STS-63 Shuttle/Mir rendezvous mission earlier this year provided a clear indication that this phase of the international Space Station Program will help us to better understand and work with Russia. Not only did NASA and the Russian Space Agency demonstrate an ability to work together, they demonstrated that solutions to difficult technical issues can be coordinated across the globe when the agencies worked effectively together to overcome a problem with the Shuttle's thrusters and enabled a successful rendezvous with the Mir.

Question 9: Perhaps the greatest challenge in the Space Station program involves the amount of spacewalking required to assemble and maintain Space Station. I understand that, according to NASA's latest estimates, it will take astronauts and cosmonauts about 888 hours of space walking to assemble Space Station and another 171 hours per year to maintain it. The estimate of spacewalking related to assembly is up 214 hours from estimates made just last year. Why such a large amount of spacewalking? Do these recent estimates raise any new concerns for you about the feasibility of Space Station?

Answer 9: Both are correct estimates. There are 648 EVA crew hours for US assembly tasks and 240 for Russian assembly tasks for a total of 888 EVA crew hours.

The scenario for maintenance EVA post-assembly complete has decreased from last year's estimate. In 1994, we told Congress the Station would require an average of 197 crew-hours per year for maintenance and the current estimate is 171. This saves us 26 hour of maintenance a year and 260 hours over 10 years.

The EVA numbers are not a concern due to the fact that they are not an excessive demand on crew members' time. Post assembly complete maintenance translates to an average of 1 EVA every 25 days. That is well within the range of the number of EVAs we know that we can safely perform per month over the fifteen-year life of the program. EVAs during assembly are also within the margins established for safe conduct of EVAs and optimum utilization of crew time.

During the assembly sequence the following average EVA rates apply:

| | |
|---|---|
| US assembly EVAs (including 15% growth factor) | 1.45 EVAs per month |
| US & Russian assembly EVAs | 1.84 EVAs per month |
| US assembly and maintenance | 2.35 EVAs per month |
| US assembly and maintenance & Russian assembly | 2.73 EVAs per month* |

* Note. The 2.73 EVAs per month is approximately an average of 1 EVA every 11 days.

We will be happy to provide a detailed briefing on our EVA management and the assumptions used in making all of our calculations. As our own experience grows with EVAs, our understanding of our capabilities increases. The Hubble Telescope servicing mission, our most EVA-intensive shuttle mission to date, demonstrated the increased maturity of our EVA capability and provided important insights for Space Station EVA planning.

Question 10: Published reports indicate that the European Space Agency will not decide on its future commitments to Space Station until late September. ESA's involvement is obviously critical since ESA will supply the European lab module. Do you have any sense that ESA's commitment to Space Station may be wavering?

Answer 10: At its March 23 meeting, the ESA Council reaffirmed Europe's determination to be an active partner in the international Space Station, and ESA Director General Luton expressed his confidence that sufficient progress is being made to finalize Europe's commitment to the program and to bring the decision process to a successful conclusion: a major role for Europe in the international Space Station.

The ESA council also confirmed ESA's contribution to the program: the Columbus Orbital Facility, an associated utilization plan, and the Ariane-5/ATV transportation system. A final decision on the European contribution will be made at the October 18-20, 1995, ESA Ministerial meeting.

Space Shuttle Budget Cuts/Safety

Question 11: Since 1992, the Space Shuttle budget has been reduced from $4 billion to $3.2 billion, with pressure for even further cuts. Last year, it was reported that both the head of the Shuttle program and the director of the Kennedy Space Center resigned in part due to concern that the push to cut costs was compromising safety.

11a: In your view, is there any factual basis whatsoever to the safety concerns supposedly expressed by these officials?

Answer 11a: Safety is always a concern to everyone involved in the Shuttle program. The cost cutting exercises that we have been involved in for the past three years have not been at the expense of safety; and, in fact, they have been accompanied by a reduced number of in-flight anomalies, ground mishaps and quality problems. The hardware and operations have matured, even as the numbers of people required to safely run the program have come down. As we look to further funding challenges in the future, we have made it clear to the projects and the review team that we will not sacrifice safety for the sake of efficiencies.

Question 11b: Can you state categorically that the Space Shuttle program is safe?

Answer 11b: There is no credible way to categorically state that the Shuttle or any other operational flying vehicle is risk free. The challenge is to minimize safety risks, and manage those that remain with operational procedures, hardware process controls, audits and inspections, and motivated trained people running the program. Effectively managing residual risk while flying complex missions and improving efficiencies continues to be the Shuttle Program s priority. The recently completed Shuttle Workforce Review was conducted with this in mind. The review showed that there are no safety holes in the program today, although there are a few areas where schedule flexibility is at a minimum. The study also found areas where further workforce reductions can be made with no significant increase in program safety risk as long as those reductions are spread over a couple of years. This would minimize disruption to ongoing operations.

Question 11c: In achieving the recent Shuttle budget cuts, what changes did NASA make?

Answer 11c: NASA has been able to reduce Shuttle costs in a number of ways. These include eliminating contractor activities that are no longer mandatory to safely fly the Shuttle, reducing the flight rate from 8 to 7 flights per year, consolidating contracts and changing contract structure. The contracts structure is changing from predominately level of effort to predominately completion form (consistent with the transition of the program from research and development to repetitive operations). Other cost savings resulted from elimination or deferral of non-mandatory upgrades, cost incentive clauses in many of the project contracts, reduced government oversight of routine, mature contractor operations and a variety of continuous improvement initiatives.

Question 11d: Can the Shuttle program withstand any additional budget cuts without raising safety concerns?

Answer 11d: The reductions recommended by the Shuttle Workforce Review do not totally resolve the budget challenges of the next few years, although they help significantly. Further savings will be possible with some changes in program plans and structure. Modifying the location of where work is performed (i.e. Palmdale vs. Kennedy Space Center, Utah vs. Mississippi, and Johnson vs. Kennedy vs. Marshall Space Centers) is a potential, long term cost saver. Also, the potential consolidation of contracts and further reductions of government management for mature, routine production and operations is under consideration. A thorough review of these options and their timing is currently underway and should help answer any questions about further cuts in the program s budget. Review results are expected by the late May timeframe.

Shuttle Replacement Vehicle

Question 12. The FY 1996 budget request includes $159 million for a new Reusable Launch Vehicle (RLV) program aimed at eventually developing a replacement launch vehicle for the Space Shuttle. What specific activities will the FY 1996 funds support?

Answer 12: Specifically, the FY 1996 budget supports the following areas:
-Continuation of the preliminary design effort for X-33,
-Continuation of full-scale development of X-34,
-Completion of flight testing for DC-XA, and
-Continuation of technology development in several areas to support an experimental flight vehicle as well as other longer range, high-payoff technology work.

Question 13: Before the end of 1996, NASA expects to decide whether to go forward with construction of an experimental vehicle -- the "X-33." What are the chief requirements that the X-33 must meet? How will the X-33 compare with the current shuttle orbiters?

Answer 13: With the X-33, we undertake to demonstrate the technology required to achieve single-stage-to-orbit (SSTO). This program integrates and expands the achievements of related efforts to produce an experimental vehicle which is both traceable at the subsystem level to a full-scale SSTO and capable of demonstrating operations costs traceable to a high-flight rate SSTO. The X-33 system must prove the concept of a reusable next-generation system by demonstrating key technology, operations, and reliability requirements in an integrated flight vehicle. NASA is working with OMB and OSTP to develop detailed technical and programmatic criteria which will provide the basis for the 1996 decision. The criteria document is nearing completion and will be subjected to and independent external review.Critical characteristics of SSTO systems, such as structural/thermal concepts, aircraft-like operations and maintenance concepts, flight dynamics, flight loads, ascent and entry environments, mass fraction, fabrication methods, etc., will be incorporated into the X-33 system and reflected in the criteria document. As a minimum, the X-33 will be an autonomous, suborbital, experimental, single-stage rocket flight vehicle. The X-33 is meant to be an experimental vehicle, a platform to demonstrate capabilities, and the Shuttle is an operational vehicle with an operational mission.

Question 14. It has been reported that, if NASA goes forward with the X-33, the Agency expects to spend about $650 million on the vehicle by the end of the decade. Is that an accurate cost estimate? Will NASA be able to pay for the X-33 and still meet its goal of cutting $5 billion from its budget over the next five years?

Answer 14: That budget estimate is generally accurate, but it should be noted that about one half of these funds are to be used for ground-based technology development work. While focus in support of the X-33, much of the ground based effort will develop technologies applicable to any next generation reusable launch vehicle system.

Question 15. Assuming that the X-33 is successfully constructed and tested, the next step is the development of an operational vehicle that serves government and industry needs. It is our understanding that NASA would like industry to share the development costs for the vehicle. What is your rough estimate of the development costs? Do you believe that industry will be willing to share the financing for the RLV development?

Answer 15: Given that we are at the very beginning of a research and development effort to answer those questions, it is difficult to predict specific outcomes. The purpose of the RLV program is to try to reduce technical and business risk to levels which would allow industry to develop the next generation launch system. If NASA, industry, and government are successful in achieving the goals we are currently setting, commercial space endeavors can be profitable, and this profitability may attract private financing.

Shuttle Privatization

Question 16: Many have suggested that NASA should consider "privatizing" the Shuttle program. The program would be turned over to a contractor, who would then sell launch services to NASA and other government and private customers.

How would this privatization concept work? Is privatization attractive to the private sector? Would privatization permit NASA to save money and still deliver the same level of services, particularly in space science? If the Shuttle program were privatized, would the private contractor acquire ownership rights to the Shuttle orbiters and related ground facilities, and, if so, what would the U.S. government get in return? What are some of the fundamental policy and legal questions that must be answered before privatization is seriously entertained?

Answer 16. Private sector involvement in operating the Shuttle program would free NASA to focus on research and development and would offer potential for improvements in efficiency and lower costs. This involvement could take several forms. While our reviews to restructure NASA are ongoing, we are also undertaking to better understand privatization and commercialization and the various options for implementing them. As the issues and options are clarified, we will share them with the Subcommittee.

Privatization of the Shuttle has been suggested. Not enough information is currently available to provide answers to your questions on privatization, however, as Space Shuttle Program restructuring options are formulated and assessed, the possibility of future privatization will be considered.

Question 17: As a prelude to later possible privatization, it has been suggested that the Shuttle contractor duties - - now spread out over three or four contractors - - be consolidated under one prime contractor. Industry seems to believe that this approach would reduce costs and workforce requirements and increase efficiency and accountability. Is NASA actively considering placing Shuttle contractor responsibilities under one prime contractor? What are some of the main issues that NASA would want to consider before going to a one prime contractor system? What are the chief advantages and disadvantages of using just one prime contractor?

Answer 17: Several options are being formulated for restructuring the Space Shuttle Program. One option is the transition of Shuttle operations to a single prime contractor. The options focus on reviewing the Program requirements and management structure in light of the increasing maturity of Shuttle operations and the fact that most of the upgrades development will be completed by FY 1998. Options include elements of civil servant downsizing, safety and mission assurance reallocation, transition of operational responsibilities to the contractors and consolidation of activities with the Space Station Program. The transition timing from today s program structure to the new structure will be key to its success. A working group has been formed, headed by the NASA Chief Engineer, to review and integrate the findings and recommendations of all the reviews and studies associated with restructuring the Space Shuttle. The results of this effort will be provided to the Associated Administrator of Space Flight who will in turn make the final recommendations to the Administrator. The results are expected in the late May timeframe.

Question 18: The development of the data system for Mission to Planet Earth - EOSDIS - is just as important as the satellite component. Every week, EOSDIS will have to collect and process the data equivalent of the entire Library of Congress. Is NASA confident that EOSDIS will be up to that challenge?

Answer 18: Yes. We are confident existing and expected technologies are capable of supporting EOSDIS requirements. Through an incremental development approach, EOSDIS will be able to handle the data generated by the MTPE satellites as each mission is launched. EOSDIS development is already proceeding to support the first launch. The prototype version of the system (Version 0) is already giving us valuable experience which we will use to improve future versions. And there is much more to come. We have designed the system to be flexible and evolvable. Specifically, we have sized the ground stations and data production facilities to receive and process all data received from all EOS satellites; the internal networks have sufficient bandwidth to transfer this data to the DAACs for permanent archive; and the DAACs have sufficient processing and archive capacity to transform the raw data into useful products. When completed, EOSDIS will be the largest civilian data system ever devised by the U.S.

Government.

In addition to using technologies that exist today, EOSDIS will take appropriate advantage of technological advances as they occur in the future, through the use of just-in-time procurements, an open system architecture, prototyping, modular design, and other features. Woven into the EOSDIS design is the ability to adapt to increases in the amount and rate of raw data input, a larger and changing user community, and an evolution in data and product requirements. Confidence in EOSDIS also comes from the community beyond NASA, including the National Research Council and the EOSDIS Advisory Panel, which have both endorsed the current approach.

Question 19: Because of the complexity of the planned data system, NASA will use a "build a little, test a little" approach to developing EOSDIS. Would you describe this approach and explain its advantages and disadvantages relative to traditional development.

Answer 19: We have been "building a little, testing a little" since 1990, which is an evolving, incremental approach that began with the current prototype system, Version 0, and will continue with Versions 1 & 2 to support the launches of the Tropical Rainfall Measuring Mission (TRMM) and the first EOS spacecraft (EOS AM-1), respectively. NASA is incrementally developing the Distributed Active Archive Centers' (DAACs) infrastructure, products and services to support seven launches between 1997 and 2000. This incremental approach ensures that the system will able to evolve in its capability, rather than having to be replaced completely every couple of years.

Traditional program development often does no more than recreate the current state of technology, while the EOSDIS architecture is specifically designed to adapt to changes (in users, requirements, and technology) so as to best serve all current and prospective users (defined and undefined). EOSDIS is being creatively designed, as stated above, not only to enable NASA's current broad vision and set of expectations but also to enable additional processes, products and services. EOSDIS will take appropriate advantage of advances in technology as the system evolves.

Space Science

Question 20: We have heard a great deal about the New Millennium approach to space exploration programs which focuses on smaller spacecraft with less expensive missions and shorter development times. How does the New Millennium compare with the old way of doing business at NASA?

Answer 20: The goal of the New Millennium Program (NMP) is to enable frequent, affordable, capable scientific missions in the 21st-century by identifying, developing and flight validating key technologies which can significantly contribute to lowering life cycle costs and increasing scientific returns. Breakthrough technologies selected from the existing technology "pipeline" -- from the ongoing technology programs of NASA, other government agencies, industry and academia -- will be developed in partnership with these organizations. Through dedicated spaceflights, critical technologies will be validated so that future science missions can take advantage of them without individually having to assume the risks inherent in their first use.

An essential element of the New Millennium process is a clear understanding of the envisioned mode for conducting scientific exploration in the next century. During the 20th century, the space science program has focused primarily on "solitary explorers." As an example, the nation's planetary exploration program -- with its initial focus on reconnaissance and preliminary characterization of the solar system -- has sent out single or dual spacecraft with complex complements of instruments to gather fundamental information about planetary surfaces, atmospheres, and the interplanetary environment. As we approach the 21st century, the fiscal environment, our technological capabilities, and our relative maturity in terms of understanding the solar system all point to a new paradigm: one that capitalizes on new technologies to enable frequent launches of low mass, low-cost spacecraft, each addressing focused sets of scientific questions.

Clearly, continued use of individual or dual spacecraft to expand our exploration frontiers is an important element of the space science program of the future. Astronomers will use individual spacecraft to continue observing all regions of the electromagnetic spectrum. Space Physicists will employ individual spacecraft to study the response of the Earth's atmosphere to solar radiative output. Planetary Scientists will use individual spacecrafts to explore Pluto, the Kuiper Belt, and beyond. Individual spacecraft can be used to characterize the surface of Mercury, and to study and monitor the outer planets and their satellites. They can be used in a series of individual launches to survey multiple asteroids and comets, and to provide sample returns from a range of possible targets.

But we also envision deployment of multiple spacecraft to analyze the more dynamic systems and processes in and beyond our solar system. Single point measurements will be insufficient to address questions concerning complex, dynamic systems. These types of questions are most appropriately addressed through time-correlated measurements at multiple locations. As an example, with a single spacecraft, it is impossible to discern with sufficient accuracy the extent to which solar tidal activities affect changes in planetary atmospheric structures. Similarly, the science community has -- for some time now -- supported concepts employing networks of landers to examine interior planetary structures and dynamics as a means to determine the size and nature of planetary cores and planetary geologic activities. Constellations of spacecraft may prove to be the most cost effective way to provide the comprehensive set of information needed to determine solar variability and its effects on Earth, to investigate global change and natural hazards. Looking beyond our Earth and solar system, optical interferometric constellations may present us with a unique and exciting opportunity to observe planets in neighboring solar systems.

Fulfilling this vision for the future will require new capabilities to reduce launch and operations costs, increase mission frequency, and enhance scientific observing and data-gathering capabilities. Capable microspacecraft and microinstruments will be required, allowing a move to the use of smaller, less costly launch vehicles. Shorter flight times and "intelligent" flight systems will be needed to reduce the number of people required to operate our spacecraft. The New Millennium Program provides for an orderly transition to this new paradigm by flight validating, in a series of technology-driven missions, those technologies which most significantly contribute to these capabilities.

The basic plan for the New Millennium Program is relatively simple and straightforward: NMP will first identify deficiencies in capabilities that preclude the immediate implementation of our scientific exploration vision. Breakthrough technology concepts that can provide affordable solutions will then be sought from the science and technology community. The highest priority technologies -- those that most significantly contribute to achieving the vision of frequent launch of exciting, affordable space and Earth sciences missions -- will be selected as candidates for development and, where necessary, flight validation.

A New Millennium Science Working Group (SWG) has been chartered to assist the program both in developing a vision of scientific exploration in the next century (discussed above) and in identifying the capabilities required to fulfill this vision. The SWG is expected to remain active throughout the course of the New Millennium Program. This will assure that the program remains focused on taking the steps necessary to achieve our scientific vision of exploration for the next century.

Integrated Product Development Teams (IPDTs) will be formed to identify candidate technologies currently under development in key technology areas. The IPDTs will establish and maintain "roadmaps" -- phased technology development plans needed to achieve the required capabilities -- for each of the key technology areas. They will determine the costs associated with advancing each technology to the point at which it is ready for validation. The teams, or subsets of the teams, will then facilitate the final development phases of those technologies determined to be of most benefit to achieving NMP objectives, and their subsequent infusion into validation flights.

The New Millennium team is beginning to evaluate candidate validation mission sets. Each mission set is composed of three to four missions occurring between 1997 and 2000. Each flight will validate a selected suite of technologies. While the primary purpose of each flight will be to validate the technologies, the method for doing so will be to design the mission to be both of scientific value and of sufficient complexity to fully exercise the technologies in the manner in which they will be expected to perform in future scientific missions. Linking the technology objectives with scientific objectives will assure close and continued interaction between technology developers and the scientific community throughout the design, development and operations phases of the missions. This is critical to ensuring that, once validated, the technologies will be readily incorporated into future scientific missions.

The decision to proceed with development of a selected mission set will depend on the overall technology richness of the mission set, its scientific value, and the future commercialization potential of the new technologies. Additionally, life cycle cost comparisons -- comparison of the cost of missions employing the new technologies vs. missions not employing the new technologies -- will be established to clearly illustrate the long term benefits of the program.

Given the decision to proceed with a given mission set, Flight Teams will be established to implement each mission. Flight Teams will work closely with the IPDTs to design the technology validation flight in a manner compatible with the technology-readiness dates, launch schedule and funding profile.

Innovative partnerships among industry, NASA centers, government agencies and academic institutions are integral to the New Millennium Program. New Millennium partners will be involved in all aspects of the program. They will participate as IPDT members, and identify and provide breakthrough technologies appropriate for NMP validation flights. They will be Flight Team members, and assume a major role in the development and fabrication of components, subsystems, systems and spacecraft for the flights. They will participate throughout the conduct of mission operations and support data processing. These partnerships -- whether it be on IPDTs or on Flight Teams -- will provide an environment conducive to the transfer of technologies and expertise to those expected to be the primary sciencecraft providers of the future.

Question 20a:  What are NASA's principle space exploration goals over the next five years?

Answer 20a:  OSS's highest priority is to complete missions under development or in operation with a disciplined commitment to live within defined cost envelopes and realize the full science potential of these missions. We also hope to initiate high priority new programs to continue the rate of discovery and knowledge and to maintain U.S. leadership in space science, which constitutes a vital transition toward a new way of doing business that is already starting to take hold.

## Current Programs

### Cassini
Significant progress has been made toward preparing the Cassini mission for its scheduled launch to Saturn in October 1997, including the recent successful completion of Critical Design Reviews for its ground system and the majority of spacecraft subsystems. FY 1996 funding will support the completion of spacecraft subsystem and instrument integration and testing, and the initiation of system-level environmental testing.

Saturn and its distinctive rings have been a source of fascination for Earth-bound astronomers for more than 300 years. Information relayed from the Pioneer and Voyager spacecraft flybys has provided some insights into this unique planetary system, while raising many more intriguing questions. As a planetary orbiter, Cassini is designed to investigate in-depth why the gaseous outer planets have evolved so much differently than the rocky inner planets like Earth, and whether Saturn's icy moons preserve a record of this formation. The mission's European Space Agency- provided Huygens probe will seek to determine whether the necessary building blocks for the chemical evolution of early life exist on Saturn's mysterious moon Titan.

### Advanced X-ray Astrophysics Facility (AXAF)
The Advanced X-ray Astrophysics program has made excellent progress over the past year. Grinding and polishing of all AXAF mirrors has been completed five months ahead of schedule and the shape and smoothness of the mirrors exceeds the required specifications. Schedule margin towards the 1998 launch has increased by two months. AXAF development will be about two-thirds complete by the end of FY 95, and about 80 percent complete by the end of FY 1996. During FY 1996, detailed design activities for the spacecraft should be completed,

and fabrication of the flight structure will begin. The spacecraft Critical Design Review is scheduled for February 1996. AXAF will study the composition and nature of galaxies, stellar objects and interstellar phenomena as well as basic issues in theoretical physics.

## Mars Surveyor
NASA's new Mars exploration strategy reaches full development in FY 1996 under the Mars Surveyor program. It consists of an initial orbiter (Mars Global Surveyor or MGS) and a subsequent series of two small missions launched every two years. With these missions, the U.S. will be able to resume the detailed exploration of Mars begun by Viking in the late 1970s. The FY 1996 budget request for Mars Surveyor will support Mars Global Surveyor instrument testing and integration with the spacecraft, and final spacecraft assembly and testing. It also will support the start of development of a small orbiter and a lander to be launched in 1998, built by contractors.

Mars Global Surveyor will carry five science instruments comprised largely of parts from the Mars Observer program aboard a small, industry-developed spacecraft that will aerobrake into its final Martian orbit using techniques refined by NASA s Magellan mission to Venus. Scheduled for launch in November 1996, it will capture much of the data that would have been obtained by Mars Observer. Following Global Surveyor will be a series of small scientific and communications orbiters. A separate series of landers will make surface measurements of the Martian climate and soil composition. In the pursuit of answers to long-held questions about the possibilities of ancient free flowing water and life on Mars, the Mars Surveyor effort should provide clues about the long- term processes of atmospheric and geologic changes on Earth.

Mars is an example on another area that will be receiving a great deal of emphasis on international cooperation. In 1993, we formed the International Mars Exploration Working Group (IMEWG). The charter of this group is to serve as discussion forum for various nations interested in mars exploration. It is developing into a strong mechanism for exchanging ideas and information, and may well facilitate actual cooperation over the long-run. Our discussion with the Russians have been particularly fruitful, and we are working to develop a joint approach to Mars exploration that will be anchored by US-Russian cooperation, and that will likely involve several other major spacefaring nations.

## International Solar Terrestrial Program (ISTP)
In FY 1996 the complete set of missions in the International Solar-Terrestrial Physics program are expected to be operational with the launches in FY 1995 and FY 1996 of FAST, SOHO, Polar, and Cluster which join Geotail and Wind in orbit to study the Sun and its influences on the Earth's space environment.

## Future Missions: OSS Strategic Planning
In the Office of Space Science or OSS, we have adopted a new outlook and a new strategy for the future of space science, one that is initially focused on the next 5 years as a crucial period. During this period, NASA s space science program has to build the scientific, technological, and international, foundation that will carry us into the next millennium.

In September 1994, this new approach to the future came together in our Space

Science Strategic Plan. Covering the period from 1995 to the year 2000, this Strategy is a marked departure from the past. It embodies a more realistic assessment of what can be accomplished over the next 5 years, and lays out a comprehensive program that reflects our new approach to doing our job. First, and above all else, we are committed to continuing to conduct a first-rate research program. We will be revising the space science program to maintain this high standard of excellence with the expectation of less outyear resources. As a result we will be working to lower the cost of any given activity, to undertake less costly and complex spacecraft, and we will do fewer things.

New mission studies during this period will focus on less costly options, with cost defined as a significant constraint early in mission definition, and with mission science objectives more precisely defined so as to contain costs. In addition, OSS will renew its emphasis on looking for opportunities to collaborate with other agencies and international partners to reduce costs and avoid duplication, and it will search for lower cost launch options wherever possible. A new matrix of missions flows from this programmatic strategy. The central characteristic of this approach is that it constitutes a balanced, world-class program of space science research that stresses smaller, less costly spacecraft, international cooperation, and technology.

**Crucial FY 1996 Budget**
The Fiscal Year (FY) 1996 budget request is especially important because it serves as our transition from the old way of doing space science to the new. It will make possible seven of our ten highest scientific priorities contained in the OSS Strategic Plan. This budget request fulfills key perishable opportunities, including the Astro-E new start with Japan which will serve as a replacement for canceled Advanced X-ray Astrophysics Facility-Spectroscopy (AXAF-S) mission and the Stratospheric Observatory for Infrared Astronomy (SOFIA) with Germany. It will also allow NASA to achieve critical program continuity in the Global Geospace Science (GGS) program through the launch of the Polar mission in FY 1996 and extension of GGS operations in the outyears.

The FY 1996 budget request provides for the continuation of the Discovery program of small, low-cost planetary missions and establishes it as a on-going, level-of-effort program. It also allows us to recover lost science resulting from earlier program cancellations, including the Astro-E mission mentioned above and an outyear new start for the U.S. lander that will fly on the European Rosetta mission as a replacement for canceled Comet Rendezvous Asteroid Flyby (CRAF) mission.

There is also room in this budget request to allow for an outyear new start for the Space Infrared Telescope Facility (SIRTF), despite the fact that OSS funding will fall by over 18 percent during the next 5 years. Also crucial to our future success is another program that is slated to begin in FY 1996, the New Millennium Spacecraft (NMS) program of technology- driven spacecraft (described above). New Millennium constitutes an important investment in technology for the future of space science. Additional information on these and other planned missions follows.

**Astro-E & Rosetta**
OSS will pursue international participation to enable missions that otherwise might

not be possible, to avoid duplication, to add science value, and to share cost with its international partners. In the case of the Japanese Astro-E mission, NASA is taking advantage of an opportunity to achieve many of the spectroscopy objectives that had been planned for AXAF-S. In the case of ESA's Rosetta mission, NASA is investigating enhancing the mission through the addition of one or more international science landers for which NASA would lead the development, in essence recapturing much of the highest priority science from the canceled Comet Rendezvous Asteroid Flyby (CRAF) mission.

## Infrared Astronomy: SOFIA and SIRTF

Space and ground-based observatories have provided a wealth of information and scientific discoveries in almost every wavelength of the spectrum. The investigation of infrared wavelengths with high sensitivity and resolution has required development of better detection instruments. In FY 1996, the NASA budget request includes funding to open a new era in infrared astronomy and begin development of two complementary missions: the Stratospheric Observatory for Infrared Astronomy (SOFIA) and the Space Infrared Telescope Facility (SIRTF). SIRTF's exquisite sensitivity and large detector arrays are designed to search for faint galaxies at the edge of the observable universe, while SOFIA will capitalize on its superior spatial resolution and spectroscopic sensitivity to study close galaxies, protostars and transient cosmic events. The two missions are described below.

## Stratospheric Observatory for Infrared Astronomy (SOFIA)

SOFIA is an infrared airborne observatory designed to replace the aging Kuiper Airborne Observatory (KAO), which has been in operation since 1974. SOFIA consists of a 2.5 meter telescope that will be carried by a specially modified, used Boeing 747 aircraft. SOFIA will be developed and operated in partnership with the German space agency, DARA. Initial operations for SOFIA will begin in late 2000. With spatial resolution and sensitivity far superior to KAO, SOFIA will enable significant advances in the study of star and planet formation, the makeup of the interstellar medium, galactic structure and evolution, and the Sun and the solar system. In addition, SOFIA will be the first NASA space science program with a significant educational outreach component built-in from the beginning. The program will build upon a very successful program of flying teachers on the KAO, by reaching out to Kindergarten to 12th grade teachers, as well as science museums and planetaria around the country.

## Space Infrared Telescope Facility (SIRTF)

Originally conceived as a $2 billion plus program, SIRTF has been restructured in cost. We now envision a spacecraft much less massive, in a different orbit, and with a revised lifetime estimate. The result is a $500 million-class mission with most of the original science intact. The FY 1996 budget request includes a significant increase for mission studies of the SIRTF observatory, in anticipation of entering development in FY 1998. SIRTF is the last of the four Great Observatories and has been the highest priority new mission (as ranked by the National Academy of Sciences) in astrophysics for many years. Recent technological breakthroughs in infrared detector technology in the United States have excited scientists and enabled an improved, less costly mission design. The SIRTF mission, planned for launch in 2002, has been vastly simplified from its original design, resulting in a dramatic five-fold reduction in life-cycle costs. SIRTF also may include a collaboration with Japan to achieve a portion of its science objectives.

## Discovery
Previously, NASA's Discovery program consisted of two Discovery missions initiated in FY 1994 and currently under development: Mars Pathfinder and the Near Earth Asteroid Rendezvous (NEAR). The FY 1996 request augments the previous budget plan by $36.6 million and provides the new funding required to continue the Discovery program.

Mars Pathfinder, scheduled for launch in December 1996 aboard a Delta II, is designed to demonstrate the technology, systems and mission elements involved in landing a series of small surface stations and rovers on Mars. The FY 1996 funding request of $35.9 million supports completion of instrument and subsystem deliveries, spacecraft integration and final spacecraft systems testing before launch.

Following its February 1996 launch, NEAR will rendezvous with its main target, the near-Earth asteroid Eros, in early 1999. The spacecraft will orbit and study Eros for at least one year. The FY 1996 funding request of $31.3 million supports completion of final spacecraft systems testing and preparation for its launch aboard a Delta II launch vehicle.

In February 1995, NASA announced the selection of the next Discovery mission -- a Lunar orbiter mission entitled Lunar Prospector. This mission was the highest rated of all proposals received in response to the recent Discovery Announcement of Opportunity. It was also the least expensive of all proposals: the total mission cost proposed, including the launch vehicle, is only $59 million. The scheduled launch date is June 1997, just a little more than 2 years from now. Three other missions were selected for further study and will compete later this year for the fourth launch opportunity.

## Explorer Program
The Explorer Program has been restructured to enable more science missions with less resources, and to enhance the role of universities in these missions. The Far Ultraviolet Spectroscopic Explorer (FUSE) mission was restructured with the goal of reducing costs and accelerating its launch schedule. This continued reduction in Explorer development costs will provide more frequent launch opportunities for NASA s Small Explorers (SMEX), Medium-Class Explorers (MIDEX), and our planned University Explorers (UNEX).

During the summer of 1995, three Explorer spacecraft are expected to launch. These include the X-ray Timing Explorer (XTE), the Fast Auroral Snapshot (FAST) small explorer, and the Submillimeter Wave Astronomy Satellite (SWAS) small explorer. XTE will provide a comprehensive record of the source of x-rays with varying intensity over time. FAST will provide high resolution data on the Earth's aurora. SWAS will provide discrete spectral data for study of the water, molecular oxygen, and carbon monoxide in dense interstellar clouds.

## Fire and Ice
While not supported in the FY 1996 budget request, NASA will also be looking to start a Pluto Flyby mission to complete the reconnaissance of the solar system, and a Solar Probe program to complete the reconnaissance of the Sun. Solar

Probe mission will allow us to get within 4 Solar Radii, 15 times closer and a lot hotter than any other spacecraft. Solar probe will answer long standing questions about what heats the extended solar corona and accelerates the solar wind.

Our current version of the Pluto mission is two 100-120 kg spacecraft that will be significantly smaller than all previous outer planet spacecraft. This mission will complete the reconnaissance of the solar system, finishing a task started over 30 years ago with our first planetary encounter of Mariner 2 at Venus. Both of these missions are envisioned in the outyears and will likely benefit from the development of new spacecraft technologies in the New Millennium program.

We have already agreed to jointly study future Pluto and Solar Probe missions with the Russians and we will be contacting other nations to foster further discussions for international collaboration on these important missions. Jointly we refer to these two missions as Fire & Ice, Fire for Solar Probe and Ice for Pluto Flyby.

**Solar Terrestrial Probes**
We hope to move forward in the next few years with a program of small, highly-focused space physics missions called Solar Terrestrial (ST) Probes. We hope to launch a series of 3 solar terrestrial probes by 2001, each with development costs of less than $100 million. They will seek answers to some very important questions about the Sun-Earth Connection and will be based on the highly successful Explorer and Discovery program lines. The first of these ST Probes, the TIMED (Thermosphere, Ionosphere, Mesosphere Energetics and Dynamics) mission will explore the middle regions of the Earth's protective atmosphere. Planned future ST Probes include the Magnetosphere Imager, which will image the Earth's magnetosphere, and HESI (High Energy Solar Imager), which will uncover some of the mysteries of solar flares (highly energetic solar outbursts that can affect spacecraft and terrestrial communications and power systems).

Question 21: Does NASA's research in telemedicine for the Shuttle and the Space Station's crews have applications to rural states in the US such as Montana and the Dakotas? If so, what are the spin-offs?

Answer 21: Telemedicine is the ability to exchange medical information and data, practice medicine, provide medical consultation, and support health care education at a distance through telecommunications and computer networks. While telemedicine was pioneered by NASA as a method for monitoring and maintaining the health of astronauts, rapid advances in computer and telecommunications technology have created enormous potential for applying telemedicine to meet medical needs here on Earth. People in rural states, where distances between medical care facilities may be great, are among the populations who stand to benefit most from an expanded role for telemedicine in our health care system.

NASA is currently developing a testbed for conducting telemedical consultations using multi-media computer platforms networked together across the Internet or Internet-like communications infrastructures. This testbed, a collaborative program with Russia called "Spacebridge to Russia", will be conducted between several U.S. medical centers and several medical sites in Moscow beginning in the Summer of 1995 and extending through the Fall of 1996. Testing and evaluation of such a system will yield an enhanced medical operations capability for the joint space flight program with Russia, and augment the development of a medical care capability for Space Station. NASA's requirements for telemedicine to maintain the health of astronauts will also enhance the delivery of health care in rural areas on earth. This testbed will also result in the reporting of findings in the literature with regard to the conduct of telemedicine. Much of NASA's earlier work in telemedicine has been or is in the process of being published in scientific and technical peer reviewed journals.

Multi-media computers, connected via the Internet or Internet-like communications infrastructure, provides a low-cost, convenient means of reliable communications from a physician's desk or examination room. Consultations can be recorded on videotape, formatted electronically, stored, and forwarded to another location for specialty consultations. This method is much more cost effective than real-time "interactive" telemedicine and represents a major departure from the direction of most domestic U.S. telemedicine programs. Real-time interactive telemedicine can also be accomplished using such a system if required. This new approach could help improve the delivery of medical care and the availability of continuing medical education in rural areas. Telemedicine over such networks could provide rural practitioners with an opportunity to consult with specialists in larger metropolitan areas, and make sophisticated specialty medical care available to otherwise isolated areas.

NASA's experience in this field is expected to yield systems for terrestrial medicine that are less expensive and more convenient than most currently used systems. This could result in cost savings in medical care and more effective and efficient delivery of medical care, particularly to remote locations. These applications can be fielded in rural America now and do not require the extensive, expensive technology being tested in other telemedicine demonstration projects. They also promise to be more easily integrated into the practice of health care in rural America.

NASA is continuing to explore and develop new telemedicine, telescience, telecommunications and Earth observation technologies and applications to improve health care delivery to rural and underserved areas and to enhance the capability for medical response to disaster-stricken areas world-wide. Specific goals and projects include development of national and international telemedicine infrastructures -- to include telecommunications and medical consultant infrastructures; telemedicine hardware, such as portable telemedicine workstations, lap-top multi-media computers, and physiological monitoring devices; development of modular, easily transportable telecommunications/telemedicine equipment packages for telemedicine applications; deployment of telemedicine equipment to rural and other areas that are underserved with regard to health care delivery; and deployment of telemedicine equipment to disaster-stricken areas to support disaster management.

Modular, easily transportable telemedicine workstations, developed to support medical operations both in space and remote locations, are expected to be incorporated into the health care delivery of rural America. These stand-alone workstations could interface with Internet or Internet-like communications networks providing rural practitioners access to specialty medical care. In addition, development of medical care systems for the International Space Station, as well as efforts in medical and biomedical research, are expected to provide many spin-offs which will be incorporated into the practice of medicine through out America. These could include: new sensors for monitoring physiological parameters; advanced imaging techniques and high speed computing; enhanced and non-invasive medical diagnostics; and virtual reality, which can be applied in surgery and medical education. All of these technologies are expected to be accessible through telemedicine, and to provide unique opportunities for both medical care and continued medical education.

Networks such as the Internet are expected to provide rural physicians access to medical expertise and continuing medical education, thereby eliminating the isolation of the medical practitioner in rural America from their colleagues. This would provide medical practitioners in rural areas of America access to continuing medical education without having to leave their practices, where they may be the only practitioner within many miles.

NASA's efforts in space exploration will continue to yield many benefits to all of humankind. Telemedicine and its applications in the space program are expected to provide many benefits to rural America, and to play a major role in the delivery of health care and continuing medical education in the 21st Century.

Question 22: If the wind tunnel initiative is eventually funded, industry will be required to contribute 10 to 20 percent of the construction costs. Is it your opinion that industry is ready at this point to provide that level of financing? What is the expected total cost of the wind tunnel construction?
What criteria would be used in choosing possible sites for the tunnels? Is it preferable to locate the two wind tunnels at the same location or to place them at different sites?

Answer 22: Industry has agreed in principle to a capital contribution of approximately 10 percent. However, a final decision will be based on the data generated by the current study, including a final cost estimate and government funding commitment. The current cost estimate is $2.28 billion.

Siting criteria are being developed as part of the study, but significant factors will include: power availability and cost, environmental and geographical suitability, and local cost sharing.

It is preferable to site both wind tunnels together.. Separating the facilities would drive costs higher both in construction and operation since a single complex would share critical staff and infrastructure.

Question 23: What went wrong with the National Aerospace Plane (NASP) program? Did its failure, as well as the failure of the "Advance Launch System" and "New Launch System" programs, provide us with any lessons on how to proceed with the new Reusable Launch Vehicle initiative?

Answer 23: The RLV program is utilizing many of the materials and analytical technologies developed by the NASP program, as well as many programmatic lessons learned. However, there are several critical differences between the two programs. The NASP program pushed the state of the art in the performance capabilities of most critical technologies. In contrast, the RLV program is aimed at demonstrating that technologies at hand, or nearly at hand, as a result of prior programs such as NASP, allow a rocket-powered, single-stage-to-orbit, reusable launch vehicle to be operable and cost-effective. Operability and cost are fundamental to the RLV program goal of reducing the cost of access to space dramatically in the first decade of the twenty-first century.

Programmatically, NASP was a joint DoD-NASA managed program with multiple funding sources and competing interests leading to a complex management structure and difficulty in establishing viable program requirements. The RLV program is an industry-led, industry/government cooperative effort with a small NASA management staff and no DoD funding or management requirement in FY 1996-2000. The RLV program requirements and success criteria are being established up front, and the criteria will be concurred in by OSTP, OMB and NASA, with review by an outside technical team. The objectives of the X-33 flight demonstration are clear: prove the operability and cost effectiveness of a rocket-powered SSTO, thereby reducing the risk for industry of developing an operational launch vehicle utilizing the demonstrated technologies. A decision gate has been established in 1996 following the initial phase of the X-33 program. At that time, the X-33 program must have demonstrated success in meeting the first set of criteria through subscale testing and detailed analysis in order for the large-scale flight demonstration phase of the program to begin.

In addition, unlike the aggressive NASP effort, the RLV program takes a step-by-step, building-block approach. The first step will be to utilize the DC-X vehicle designed, built and flown under DoD auspices. This vehicle will be upgraded and flight-tested in 1996 with critical new technologies (e.g., composite and advanced metallic reusable cryogenic tanks and composite vehicle structures) and a small operations team. The X-34 small booster will fly in 1997-1998 using many of the new technologies and a small operations team, and will demonstrate the effectiveness of the streamlined cooperative management structure. The X-33 large-scale demonstrator will take advantage of the technical and programmatic lessons learned in the prior efforts and will fly in 1999, proving that a large-scale SSTO RLV can be designed, built and flown reliably and at far lower cost than current launch vehicles.

Question 24: Are you confident that NASA's FY 1996 budget gives adequate support to next-generation subsonic, supersonic, and hypersonic aeronautics research? What steps is NASA taking to ensure that the aeronautics research is relevant to the needs of the aerospace industry?

Answer 24: NASA Aeronautics ensures that its program is relevant and responsive to its customers and stakeholders needs through a variety of mechanisms. Industry partners are involved in the identification, development, and execution of programs to ensure that those programs reflect market realities and customer priorities. External advisory committees, composed of leaders from industry, academia, and other government agencies, monitor relevance by reviewing program priorities and progress. Industry representatives from all levels interact constantly with NASA researchers and managers. NASA's technological relevance is also illustrated by the large number of NASA/industry cooperative programs and by the willingness of industry to enter into cost-sharing arrangements with NASA. Efforts are underway to further strengthen this important government/industry alliance. Industry is involved in the National Science and Technology Council's (NSTC) efforts to develop national aeronautics R&D priorities. In addition, industry will be involved in the development of an integrated national strategy and priorities assessment for civil aeronautics, as requested by the Office of Management and Budget in the FY 1996 budget passback.

In light of the constrained budgetary environment, NASA has worked closely with our partners to ensure the FY 1996 request is the right budget required to meet the technology needs of our customers. The level of funding in the President's FY 1996 budget request, therefore, provides a proper level of support for the next generation of subsonic, supersonic, and hypersonic aeronautics research. In order to maintain NASA's technology commitments to industry and ensure that competitive aeronautics technologies for the next generation of aircraft are developed, it is essential those technology development programs be funded at the requested annual levels.

## Russian Contribution Summary

| Element Name | Weight (lbs) | Flight (9/28 Seq) | Purpose |
|---|---|---|---|
| Service Module | 50,706 | 1R - 4/98 | Core module of Russian Segment with full GN&C, Propulsion, Crew Systems, C&T, etc. systems. |
| Soyuz | 15,102 | 2R - 5/98 | Crew Transfer and Return vehicle. |
| Universal Docking Module | 15,432 | 3R - 6/98 | Module to support the docking of multiple elements. (2 axial and 4 radial ports). Also contains their batteries for electrical power. |
| Docking Compartment | 8,598 | 4R - 7/98 | A pressurized volume which interfaces several Russian Elements and is capable of performing the airlock function for EVA. |
| SPP-1 | 15,432 | 5R - 11/98 | Lower section of truss to support Russian Solar Power Arrays. Also houses the 6 Gyrodynes for nonpropulsive attitude control. |
| SPP-2 | 15,432 | 6R - 2/99 | Upper segment of truss and solar arrays. Supports one or two thruster modules. One delivered on this flight with additional modules delivered as required. (Two modules tentatively scheduled for flight, 12R - 11/00 and one on 14R - 10/01) |
| SPP Solar Arrays (4) | 5,732 | 7R - 5/99 | Addition of solar arrays (4) Additional arrays on 14R - 10/01 |

## Russian Contribution Summary

| Element Name | Weight (lbs) | Flight (9/28 Seq) | Purpose |
|---|---|---|---|
| Research Modules #1 | 20,944 | 8R - 9/99 | Modules to support science experiments. They can be detached and replaced as required to support new experiments. |
| #2 | 5,432 | 10R - 6/00 | |
| #3 | 15,432 | 13R - 8/01 | |
| Docking and Stowage Mdle | 15,432 | 9R - 1/00 | Pressurized module to allow docking of Russian elements and volume to store material. |
| Life Support Module | 15,432 | 11R - 10/00 | Module to provide specific life support functions to complement Service Module and US elements. At assembly complete this will be the primary crew support module on Russian segement. |
| Cargo Transfer Vehicle | | | Will be scheduled as required to provide cargo and propellants to support station operations |
| Progress M (Current) | 15,705 | | |
| Progress M2 (Planned upgrade) | 25,684 | | |

Responses to written questions submitted by Sen. McCain resulting from the March 1, 1995, hearing.

Question: Mr. Goldin, in its FY 1996 budget request NASA has included monies for the X-34 Reusable Launch Vehicle (RLV) program. My understanding is that this program is designed to address an emerging commercial space market in the 1,000-2,000 pound payload range. In addition, I understand that the X-34 will contribute to NASA's other major Reusable Launch Vehicle initiative, the X-33. In light of these considerations, please respond to the following:

- What is NASA's assessment of the commercial market potential of a X-34 space launch vehicle capable of placing payloads in the 1,000-2,000 pound class into low-Earth orbit?

- What are the benefits to be derived from the X-34 program with respect to technologies needed for the successful execution of the X-33 and the government-industry management relations (e.g. the investment of private capital) that will be needed for the X-33?

Answer: NASA does not possess the expertise to assess the market for small satellite launches. Our selected partners, as part of their X-34 proposal, conducted a market survey which identified every satellite which will be built over the next ten years and assessed the likelihood of their X-34 derived commercial vehicle capturing that market. While the results of that market study are proprietary, we can note that their evaluation of the market was apparently sufficiently positive to justify their $100 million investment in the program.

The X-34 program serves three important functions in the RLV program: It will quickly and firmly establish small, fast-paced, industry-led program management within the RLV program; it will flight test a number of technologies which have been developed subsequent to the development of the Space Shuttle, but have not previously been flight qualified in a space launch system; and it will provide early operations experience with an <u>economic</u> reusable launch vehicle. The first of these is an especially important point which is too easily overlooked. NASA has limited previous experience managing in this manner; without the X-34 program, the X-33 will be our first chance to learn how to conduct a fast paced, industry lead program. We believe the management risk to X-33 will be significantly reduced as a result of the experience gained on X-34. Because the X-34 will be the first reusable, all-composite space launch system, we expect it will prove essential to the RLV program both by flight qualifying that technology in a space launch environment and by providing early operational experience on an all-composite reusable vehicle.

The investment of private capital for X-33 does nothing directly on X-34, although the successful attraction of private capital to the X-34 effort certainly offers a model for the X-33 and any subsequent vehicle programs. Establishing that a government-industry partnership can effectively manage such a program lends credibility to the belief that we can do the same on the much larger X-33.

Responses to written questions submitted by Sen. Dorgan resulting from the March 1, 1995, hearing.

Question 1: It is my understanding that the Gravity Probe-B project has been funded by NASA since 1984. This project has undergone about 17 studies and reviews to validate its scientific merit. It is further my understanding that the FY 1996 budget request has recommended that this project be put on hold, pending another study to determine its merit. Can you tell me why this particular project needs additional study? Have previously unknown concerns emerged about the project.

Answer 1: A long period of time has lapsed since the Gravity Probe-B (GP-B) mission was begun. We have recently re-examined and restructured all of our science missions. In this vein, we have asked the National Research Council to review GP-B's scientific merit, technical feasibility and value compared to other programs. Thus, NASA is simply subjecting the mission to the same process as all other science missions.

Question 2: Has the Gravity Probe-B project progressed according to schedule towards its October 2000 launch date?

Answer 2: Development of the Gravity Probe-B mission was initiated in FY 1993 as successor to the Shuttle Test Of Relativity Experiment (STORE) program already underway. Total program development costs for the combined GP-B/ STORE program were estimated at $531 million in support of a planned launch in September 1998. The mission was rebaselined in the FY 1995 President's Budget to a level-of-effort program which limited annual funding to approximately $50 million per year. Funding reserves were added beyond FY 1999 as a placeholder to support a launch delay to as late as FY 2003. Total development costs were re-estimated at $606 million -- an increase of $75 million over the previous estimate.

Question 3: How is the Gravity Probe-B project doing with respect to its costs? Has the project experienced any cost overruns or other budgeting concerns?

Answer 3: This cost growth has since been eliminated by restructuring the program. The STORE program has been eliminated by transitioning instrument development from a prototype to a protoflight program, thus eliminating planned Shuttle performance tests and reducing ground testing. Reduced program content has also allowed acceleration of the planned launch to October 2000. Total development cost are now estimated at approximately $475-500 million, a net reduction of about $100 million over the previous program scenario. Cost and schedule performance against the new program baseline has thus far been satisfactory. All major planned activities are currently being conducted on time and within available funding levels.

Responses to written questions submitted by Sen. Stevens resulting from the
March 1, 1995, hearing.

Question 1: What advantages does the Wind Tunnel program provide to
the United States?

Answer 1: The United States' share of the world civil aviation market has
eroded dramatically in the last 20 years as the European Airbus Industrie
Consortium introduced a family of commercial aircraft that captured over 35% of
the global market. This is largely attributable to the strong support of Airbus by
European governments, including subsidies, research, and investments in
infrastructure, which allows Airbus to offer aggressively priced, technically
innovative products. The world civil aircraft market is forecast to be $1 trillion over
the next 20 years and Airbus is targeting at least 50% of that market, representing
a potential substantial revenue loss to the U.S.

It is critical that U.S. industry enter the next century with the tools
necessary to remain the dominant force in an extremely competitive marketplace.
The Europeans have built six new state-of-the-art wind tunnels in the last 15
years; with one exception, the U.S. inventory of wind tunnels is between 30 and
40 years old. Although domestic companies currently test in the more advanced
European tunnels, industry is very concerned over the loss of proprietary data and
possible future access problems. The National Wind Tunnel Complex would be on
line in time to impact the emerging $1 trillion market by providing domestic aircraft
makers with the best aeronautical ground test facilities in the world.

Question 2: What problems prevented NASA from reporting to Congress
NASA's plan to implement the program by the deadline of 1 March, 1995, as
required in last year's appropriations report language?

Answer 2: The appropriations report language spelled out conditions for
the appropriation of $400 million for new aeronautical facilities. Among these
conditions were an Administration FY 1996 budget request of at least $400 million
and a comprehensive plan and strategy for the wind tunnels. The Administration
did not include the wind tunnels in its FY 1996 budget request; a
government/industry team is currently studying the wind tunnel concept. Until that
study is complete and data can be carefully evaluated, it would be premature to
either rescind or augment the current funding. The Administration plans to make a
decision whether to proceed with the wind tunnels as part of the FY 1997 budget
process. The comprehensive plan called for in the appropriations report language
will be developed and submitted to Congress at the appropriate time in that
process.

Question 3: Have you considered the resources of the University of
Alaska, including its supercomputer, in your site selection analysis?

Answer 3: Site selection activities are not being conducted until the
Administration decides, during the FY 1997 budget process, whether to proceed
with the wind tunnels. However, the site selection process will allow ample
opportunity for each state to put forward its best proposal, including existing
complementary technical infrastructure.

Question 4: As you may be aware, the State of Alaska is committed to the construction of a polar launch site on Kodiak Island. Are you aware of any impediments to NASA's use of that launch site?

Answer 4: NASA delegates selection of launch site to its launch service contractor. The recent Med-Lite launch service Request for Proposal, for example, did not specify any particular launch site; rather it stated mission performance requirements and left the location of the launch site to the service provider. NASA is also working with Alaska Aerospace Development Corporation (AADC) personnel to help AADC define its requirements for the provision of range safety services. At the request of AADC Goddard Space Flight Center personnel attended the AADC 35% design review at the end of last year, and NASA continues to be involved with AADC as well as the other emerging State Spaceport Authorities.

Question 5: Will NASA help Alaska obtain the Range Safety System it requires on a true direct cost basis?

Answer 5: In response to Alaska's request, NASA has offered to provide the mobile range safety function located at the Wallops Flight Facility, which is currently used to support various sounding rocket campaign as well as provide range services to private sector companies under the Commercial Space Launch Act (CSLA). The mobile range safety function consists of several vans along with additional equipment and personnel. NASA has been discussing provisions of this function to the Alaska Aerospace Development Corporation (AADC), which is the entity responsible for the launch site at Kodiak. As required by the CSLA the equipment and personnel would be provided on a direct cost, non-interference basis. Direct cost is defined by the CSLA as those costs unambiguously associated with the commercial launch effort and which would not be borne by the government in the absence of a commercial launch effort. Any charges to AADC for use of the mobile range safety function would be consistent with the CSLA definition which has been fully incorporated into NASA's internal financial management instructions and is routinely applied to all services provided pursuant to the CSLA. We have discussed this approach with AADC.

Question 6: What are your plans to protect and enhance the sounding rocket program, which is vital in studying the middle atmosphere, unreachable by any other means?

Answer 6: As a consequence of accommodating a flat budget, the Office of Space Science has focused over the past year on reducing operational costs of the program without sacrificing the reliability of the delivery systems and the requirements of the scientific community. As a result, sounding rocket missions will now be conducted in the same fashion that balloon campaigns are done. Science will continue to drive the selection of missions and the location of future launches. Missions will be prioritized and selected to be launched in groups from a particular site. The traditional approach of supporting all highly rated requests for flight at multiple sites in a given year is no longer viable with a flat budget. Missions will no longer be launched from as many sites. The goal of this policy is to absorb a flat budget while maintaining a healthy launch rate.

3.

We will continue these efforts to make the program more efficient. In the long term, flight rates may decrease with the continuation of a flat budget.

Question 7: NASA has adopted as every other year schedule for launching sounding rockets from a particular range, or site. This schedule has wreaked havoc with the research programs of individual scientists. How do you propose to compensate for this loss in research opportunities, and the needless delay in graduate students careers?

Answer 7: In order to accommodate a flat operational budget for the sounding rocket program in future years, the Agency had to determine where funds could be saved when opportunities presented themselves. For example, when Poker Flat Research Range operations and maintenance contract was up for renewal in 1994, the contract language to which both parties agreed incorporated three years of normal operations and two years in which the range would be in a caretaker status. We realize that this imposes hardship at the range in maintaining a qualified crew, but this was an opportunity to adjust the new contract to the budget realities known to us last fall. We are well aware that imposing schedule constraints will create difficulties for graduate students. A diminished capability to support sounding rocket operations will have a dampening effect on some future science activity. However, the realities of the budgetary constraints require conducting operations at multiple launching sites in a manner which maximizes the scientific and technical return per dollar.

Question 8: NASA is considering implementing a voucher system for sounding rocket research missions. What is your specific position about this plan and will you provide details about implementation and schedule?

Answer 8: The voucher program was originally conceived as a demonstration effort to be tested by the Office of Space Access and Technology (Code X). Because their budget could only sustain one sounding rocket flight, the Office of Space Science (Code S) was asked to provide five additional flights out of its peer-reviewed science program. To date, there have been no formal volunteers. The Space Physics Division as the result of a NASA Research Announcement this past year was unable to obtain any successfully peer-reviewed science proposals where there was an interest by the science investigators in participating. We currently know of two investigators who might have an interest in participation if their new instruments go through successful qualifying flights by conventional means. Neither of these payloads would be ready to fly until FY 1996 owing to payload development schedules and operational considerations. We will continue our efforts to locate investigators interested in participating in the demonstration program.

Question 9: Both the Senate and the House have passed legislation to complete the upgrade of Poker Flat Research Range. How do you propose to accomplish this important objective, without jeopardizing the funding for the sounding rocket-borne science mission, and satellite science missions?

Answer 9: NASA worked an agreement in 1992 with the University of Alaska, Geophysics Institute which ensured that a balanced upgrade plan would be put in place. Prominent among the highest priority work to be done was establishing a safe range in which to conduct our launches. NASA is satisfied with the level of upgrades at the rocket range insofar as our operations are now conducted in much safer facilities than existed only two years ago. NASA does not propose to invest more funds in the range given the budgetary situation and limitations on our capacity for conducting future remote campaigns. We were given some assurance from the Director of the Geophysics Institute that he was satisfied with the level of NASA's contributions to date.

○

ND - #0037 - 210323 - C0 - 229/152/8 [10] - CB - 9780656714360 - Gloss Lamination